I0145210

Padre Pro

Mexican Hero

Padre Pro

Mexican Hero

By
Fanchón Royer

Illustrated by James J. Fox

HILLSIDE EDUCATION

Copyright © 2019 by Hillside Education

Originally published by P.J. Kenedy & Sons, 1963

All rights reserved. No part of this publication may be
reproduced in whole or in part, stored in a retrieval system
or transmitted in any form or by any means, electronic,
mechanical, photocopying, recording, or otherwise, without
prior written permission of the publisher.

Cover image *Execution of Miguel Pro*, used by permission:
Historic Images / Alamy Stock Photo

Cover and interior book design by Mary Jo Loboda

ISBN: 978-0-9991706-8-7

Hillside Education
475 Bidwell Hill Road
Lake Ariel, PA 18436
www.hillsideeducation.com

Contents

Padre Pro

Mexican Hero

The Boy Who Didn't Go to School

"MIGUEL Agustín" called the Mine Bureaus new agent, "will you please dig into the closed files for a couple of cases titled Amalgamated Silver and Santa Marta Mining? I'll need to run over them before this afternoon's meeting."

His young clerk looked up amiably from the counterful of fat folders he was sorting. "Certainly, Papá. But they won't take much digging. Cases 105 and 110 in Justified Claims, 1901, coming right up!" he laughed as he slid off his stool and crossed the old-fashioned office to an ancient cabinet

Watching him swiftly whip out the wanted material, Don Miguel Pro was marveling, as usual, at his 15-year-old's amazing memory. But then he sighed. It was really a shame that memory wasn't being used in study toward a professional career. In permitting his clever eldest son to cheat himself of even a high-school education hadn't he sadly failed his parental duty?

The bright-eyed youngster with the wide, humorous mouth dropped the case histories on his father's desk, saying: "Just don't let that meeting drag on too long, Papá. This is the big night, you know. And I've got the girls, even the little fellows, ready to make your and Mamá's anniversary a real fiesta."

Don Miguel's frown melted into a fond smile. "Don't worry, son. I'll run the gentlemen out in good time."

One of the reasons why young Miguel had not received the proper formal education was his tremendous attachment to his family. Two times he had been sent away to city boarding schools from this isolated Zacatecan mining camp, but he had been so miserable over the separation from his parents, from his adoring sisters and brothers that his health was endangered. So they had had to bring him home.

At one point, Don Miguel had resigned his mine managership in order to move his children near good schools, but then had come this government appointment to keep them in rude little Concepción del Oro. It just had been too good a post to refuse. Whereupon, in this year, 1907, Miguel had become his excellent assistant. Even so, he wasn't fooling his father that he was actually interested in anything about the mining industry—save the poor, overworked miners to whom he was forever carrying his mother's gifts of food, medicines, and clothing. No, his invaluable services in the office were simply owed to the obedience he always showed to his parents. But what, then, was he going to do with his future? Well, sighed Don Miguel again, he must certainly see to it that his failure with Miguel's schooling wasn't repeated in the cases of the younger boys. . . .

If the ambitious and surprisingly well-rendered concerto by the Pro family orchestra had won a buzz of most gratifying compliments, its melodious standbys, "Over the Waves," "Mixteca," and "Zacatecas," had rung the rafters with the applause of parents and guests. As he took his bows, Director Miguel Agustín knew that his orchestra had done itself proud this night. So he motioned to his older sisters Concepción and Luz, and his younger sisters Ana María and Josefina, to rise for their bows.

Only young Edmundo and the babies, Humberto and Roberto, had still to master a musical instrument under his teaching. And even they had perfectly committed to memory the verses he had written for them to recite in honor of their parents. Their part of the program would come now, then the poems by the others and presentation of the home-made gifts, and, lastly, the gay charades Miguel was so clever at thinking up. Much better than the applause was the sight of Mother Josefa's eyes ashine with happy tears; Father Miguel's, glinting with pride and approval. Miguel would have hated the very thought of exile, for any reason whatsoever, from this closely knit clan and its flattering admiration of his talents.

However, this life that the Pros had lived so long was due to undergo a radical change. The very next morning, dining a quiet half-hour in the office, his father announced: "Your mother and I have decided she must take the children to Saltillo for the coming school year. Neither of us can bear

Mother Josefa's eyes shone with happy tears, Father Miguel's with pride and approval.

the prospect of none of our sons having a good education. Moreover, today Concepción del Oro can't produce a single tutor such as we were lucky enough to hire for the primary instruction you and the older girls received. Ana María and Josefina will attend high school and Edmundo a good grammar school. . . ."

"But, Papá . . ."

"I know. It'll be very hard being parted from my family, but there's no other way to handle this problem. And besides, I can take the train up to Saltillo each weekend to see you."

"To see *us,* Papá? I'm to go, too? To leave the office?

"You're to accompany your mother, yes, since she and your sisters certainly can't be sent off to a strange city without a man's protection. But you'll still be my clerk. I shall mail you

the records for classifying and memorizing, then pick them up along with your notations on my weekends with you. It shouldn't be a difficult adjustment."

"But how about you, Papá? Won't you be awfully lonely those other five days? Shouldn't you keep either Concepción or Luz or both of them here to take care of you?"

"Impossible, son. Your mother can't be asked to run so big a household without their help. Anyway, I don't hold with girls of their ages being parted from their mothers. I'll make out, and I might even get a transfer that will let me join you before too long. But, if not, you'll be coming home to me for the long vacations."

Distressing as it was to be leaving their father, Miguel found himself more than a little relieved not to be losing his most skillful musicians. So long as he needn't be deprived of his mother, his sisters, and the music they made together, he could look forward zestfully to a break in Concepción del Oro's monotony. He was really eager to learn another way of life, to hear Saltillo's famed band concerts while participating in evening promenades about the park, and to be a part of a sophisticated city society.

But as it turned out, his father's reason for sending bim to Saltillo was the first justified. For hardly were they established in their house when serious trouble descended upon it. Thirteen-year-old Josefina fell desperately ill. Then indeed did Doña Josefa have cause to thank heaven that her Miguel was by her side to aid her in this terrifying misfortune. But, even so, they could not save Josefina. Her death was the worst blow the Pros had yet received.

After Josefina had left them, Miguel spent his every hour trying to make this tragic time a bit easier for his mother, the three remaining girls, and the three small brothers.

To the latter he became a true second father who commanded their respect and obedience as he had his sisters' cooperation in his childhood's games and schemes. Then, as their sorrow began to soften, he resumed their musical evenings, once again led their play, and cracked the little jokes that coaxed their smiles. And meanwhile, he never failed to keep abreast of Don Miguel's cases. His father had only to write and ask about any action to find an intelligent analysis of it awaiting his next trip to Saltillo.

All the same, it would seem that somewhere about this time Miguel became acquainted with loneliness. Never before had he felt the lack of outside friends. But now, at sixteen, he must have missed a special pal, because one day he surprised Concepción by declaring, "You'll have to be the friend I've never had."

And so it was to be. These two went everywhere together. She heard all about his indifference to mining or any other commercial enterprise; how he couldn't make up his mind as to what he wanted to do with his life. And though Concepción certainly enjoyed her inclusion in the enthusiasms he did have—music, poetry, play acting—it sometimes worried her that they were all such short-range interests. She was correct in assuming these things were only a passing fancy for Miguel. He never even considered a theatrical career because to folk of the Pros' class and devout Catholicism, the shoddy Mexican stage of 1907 was one of the unthinkable occupations.

From Concepción's point of view their closeness did have one painful aspect. All too often it made her the victim of her brother's many and varied practical jokes. And it wasn't much consolation that, after shamelessly embarrassing her, he innocently expected to soothe her outraged feelings with his, "But aren't you my *friend*?"

There was the time they had been strolling about the plaza, looking for, according to Miguel, some pretty girls newly arrived in Saltillo. But they had seen no lovely strangers, and Concepción was getting tired. She suggested it was time to be going home, and, somewhat to her surprise, he agreed. They were halfway home before she became suspicious. That was when, halting before a perfectly strange house, he announced, "I've this little call to make," as he banged the heavy brass knocker.

"But on whom? We don't know these people!" she protested nervously. His reply was only an altogether too familiar impish grin, as he banged the knocker again.

The door was opened by the master of the house, who seemed as puzzled by their presence as was Concepción herself. She was absolutely certain that neither she nor Miguel had ever so much as seen this man on the street. But her brother was greeting him heartily—which left the befuddled householder no choice but to invite them into his parlor. And the next thing Concepción knew, she was sitting on the edge of a chair, listening to Miguel's preposterous explanation.

"You must be so good as to pardon us, Señor," he was beaming, "but my sister here was so enchanted by that image of the Virgin, which she noticed as we were passing your window, that she begged me to inquire whether you might be willing to sell it to us."

The scarlet-faced Concepción hadn't even seen an image! However, following the glances of her impossible brother and their bewildered host, she found herself looking upon a statue of the Virgin so overdressed and altogether so gawdy that she could barely hold back a hysterical giggle. It was all she could do to keep quiet as she heard the owner of this atrocious statue saying that it was a treasured family heirloom. "With many regrets, I must therefore tell you, young man, that I couldn't bring myself to part with it—that is, for less than five hundred pesos."

"Ah, but a thousand thanks for this great favor, Señor. I assure you," Miguel rattled on, "that nothing remains but to inform our parents of such a remarkable bargain. They will doubtless be delighted to make my sister's dream come true." This terrible Miguel! Now he was giving the still somewhat confused gentleman their address, with street and number both so rapidly invented that there wasn't the least hesitation in his flow of words.

When Miguel had ushered the furiously humiliated Concepción into the street, before she could utter a word, he remarked brightly: "After such a fine rest we might as well get back to the plaza. The beautiful strangers must certainly have turned up by now."

But Concepción had no intention of taking this joke lying down. "And just what do you think Mamá will have to say about these goings-on?"

"What do you mean—Mamá? Aren't we *friends?* You just keep quiet now and come along with me. I'll buy you an ice cream."

But Miguel himself was too amused to keep this incident from their mother. And he told it with so sharp an imitation of both their host's amazement and Concepción's horror that Josefa couldn't help laughing. After which she could hardly give Miguel the scolding her ruffled daughter insisted he deserved.

But he didn't always get off so easily. One of these times was when he sent an Indian peddler to their doorway while Concepción was bidding farewell to some tea party guests, girls of Saltillo's most prominent families. The man was carrying a huge basket heaped with the vulgar article of food known as pig cracklings, which are made by toasting the thick, dried skin of the pig.

Boldly shoving his greasy product into the circle of young ladies, he stated, "Don Miguelito has sent a gift of her favorite dish to the Señorita Concepción."

His announcement started some most unladylike laughing and teasing of poor Concepción. Her hasty protests that this was merely another of Miguel's stupid jokes did little to repair the damage to her pride. Moreover, this time even Josefa was irritated. When Miguel finally put in an appearance, he was spared from neither side, but, as usual, he had a quick reply.

"Darling Mamácita, don't you see? I only did it to take those silly girls down a peg. They were surprised into a laugh and had to drop their society airs." Then he caught Josefa up in a bear hug as he promised to try to keep his humor under better control in the future, or at least to avoid hurting his sister's feelings.

2

The Brewing Storm

DON MIGUEL had made a hundred round trips on the dirty little trains running between Concepción del Oro and Saltillo. But he couldn't keep up these visits to his family very long now that the miners were becoming so troublesome. If they started to riot out of hatred for the mineowners, who worked them so hard for less than a living wage, then Don Miguel's duties as government agent would nail him to his post. Besides, rioters would be sure to stop, if not destroy, the trains. Even if violence could be avoided, it seemed only right to Doña Josefa that her husband now should have the full-time aid and company of his son.

So Miguel said good-by to the orchestra, the charades, and the city gaiety he had enjoyed so much and returned to Concepción del Oro. He carried his father the word that the others would also be coming home for good after the closing of their second school year. His mother believed that in such threatening times they should all be together.

If to Miguel the vacations seemed very far away, he bore his loneliness in silence as he resumed the monotonous office routine. Then, since the long evenings in their empty house were hardest of all, he decided to spend them teaching himself English and French. He fell to work with a will, greatly helped by his fine memory.

And the next thing he knew the whole family was home again. If this was a blessing for the tired father, it was pure delight for the brother. Once again the house rang with music and laughter. Once again there was an admiring audience for his imitations, his boredom-banishing tomfoolery.

His mischief, though constant, never led him to disobey his parents' commands. And because they knew him worthy of their trust, he was sometimes allowed to escort the girls to local entertainments. It was on one of these evenings that he was given the most impressive possible proof of the positive value of obedience.

As he and Concepción were returning from a show along the mine-railway tracks, they saw speeding toward them a trainload of molten metal from the furnaces.

"Come along—and hurry," said Miguel, catching her elbow. "We've got to be clear over in the field before it gets here. Papá doesn't want us anywhere near these carriers." They therefore bustled, not only off the right of way, but deep into the bordering field before turning to watch the glowing cargo dramatically streaking through the night. Then Concepción suddenly screamed. There was a fiery explosion as one of the cars tipped over.

"Chihuahua!" exclaimed Miguel, "Exactly where we'd have been standing if we'd just stepped off the tracks!"

Now there came a grinding of brakes, and, when the

train stopped, the engineer leaped from the cab to inspect the damage. But he must have been drowsy because, to their horror, he lost his footing.

"Look!" yelled Miguel, "he's gone headfirst into that mess of liquid metal!" And even before they heard the poor fellow's agonized screams, Miguel was running toward the frightful scene. But it was no use. There was no way to reach, let alone pull the man out.

Then, useless though they knew it to be, they ran for help. All who gathered at the site of the accident agreed that nobody could have rescued the driver after his first slip.

Another sort of explosion now erupted in ordinarily quiet Concepción del Oro. During Mexico's Independence fiesta, September 15-16, the long-dreaded riot broke loose. The miners' resentment had been aggravated by the holiday drinking. Amid rageful shouts of "Exploiters!" a mob was soon milling about the Mine Bureau.

"But why come here?" Miguel asked his father as they stood looking down upon the scene from their upstairs living quarters. "They all know you were never an owner."

"But you are forgetting that it is I who hold what they are after, son, the property titles. Thank God I had that impulse to bring them up here. Because this is really trouble."

"But what do they mean by threatening *you*? There must be plenty of your old friends out there who know what a kind superintendent you always were. How can they forget how often you helped them out with money from your own pocket? And look at all Mamá is still doing for their families. Why, I've heard them call her their 'merciful angel' many a time."

"Yes, and they've always been devoted to you, too, but you can hear for yourself . . ."

"Those titles! We want those titles we've sworn to do away with!"

As the first rocks and gunshots broke the office windows, Don Miguel announced: "I'm going out to face them, try to quiet them down. Those who ever worked for me will surely give me a hearing, maybe even help me calm down the rest. Otherwise, as soon as they discover that the files are gone, they'll certainly come swarming up here. At all costs I've got to keep them out of our home."

"No, oh no, dearest," pleaded Doña Josefa, while the girls burst into tears. "Can't you hear how drunk they are? They're not responsible. One of them might easily pull a pistol and shoot you before you can say a word."

"She's right, Papá," declared Miguel. "Surely you won't help them to kill or hurt you uselessly."

In the end they won the argument. Don Miguel remained inside, listening with growing concern to the destruction taking place below, the suddenly increased frenzy of the yells that showed the miners had discovered the absence of the files. Now the shrieks were for "young Miguel," because they knew he was in charge of the files.

At this, he undertook to make a game of their peril for the reassurance of his mother and the girls. "Only hear how I'm acclaimed!" he exclaimed. "Poor me, to be so innocent and yet so roundly hated." And so saying he snatched up his guitar and began to sing some of his noisiest songs. When his father snapped for him to be quiet, he disappeared into the dining room and returned with a platterful of candy for his sisters.

To their vast, if short-lived, relief, the raiders began to move off into the next street. Spying through the shutter cracks, Miguel reported: "Now they're attacking the Protestant chapel. Oh, oh, here they come back again."

It was true. Within minutes the mob was again boiling about the office, and it looked as though they were preparing to assault the house. So while Doña Josefa and her daughters prayed to the Virgin for protection, father and son shoved the heavy furniture against the door and prepared to defend their home.

But at the very instant that the shooting and rock bombardment turned upward, there came a pounding of horses' hoofs over the yells, crashes, and shots. Miguel tore back to his post at the window.

"The *Rurales!*" he cried. It was the far-famed and mightily feared Civil Guard, which kept the so-called order for the proprietors guaranteed by President Porfirio Díaz. Momentarily stricken dumb, Miguel watched these guards gallop upon and right over the rioters. To their horror, Miguel and his father saw the miners dropped by the blazing government guns. "Oh, the poor things," he choked in consternation, "they're being killed like dogs!"

Thus did this riot meet an abrupt end, but in circumstances more dreadful than either Don Miguel or his son believed were possible. They had too long sympathized with these men who went down into the earth to labor long hours for pathetically poor pay to be able to resent their rebellion. Besides, they knew that meeting violence with violence was no solution.

"This riot has been put down, but nothing has been settled," said Don Miguel, shaking his head sadly. "There will be other riots, other deaths. May God help us all, the miserable miners as well as the Pros."

He and his father saw the miners dropped by the blazing government guns.

At the height of the danger various members of the family had made vows to heaven to be fulfilled if they were spared. Miguel's, which was not to have a girl friend for a full year, seems to have turned out to be harder than he had foreseen.

As he approached his eighteenth birthday, he began to act exceedingly strange. Almost overnight this merry son and brother fell moodily silent, or decidedly short-tempered, when pestered by the other children. Worst of all, he was now openly bored by the devotions he had loved all his life. Ever since his First Communion, he had received every First Friday. He heard Mass each Sunday and Holy Day. He never missed the family Rosary led by his devout mother every evening. Nor did he think of these practices as merely his obligation. They made him happy and filled him with confidence. But he certainly didn't regard himself as pious. And, truth to tell, no one had ever suggested that he was. In fact, there must have been many who, judging by his constant clowning, took him for a quite lightheaded youth.

Perhaps Doña Josefa alone knew his whole heart— its great tenderness for the Faith, as well as for his family. Thus it was a heavy blow to see that heart suddenly harden. Something was very wrong with Miguel.

Doña Josefa fastened the last stitch into the chalice veil she had embroidered for the parish. She had been praying as she worked for the wisdom to save her eldest boy and his good influence upon the others. If she might be granted this blessing, she wouldn't ask to know the whys and wherefores of his present spiritual troubles.

She folded her finished needlework into a neat little square. "One of you," she said to her daughters, "will please wrap this up and tell Miguel to take it to the pastor for me."

"You mean—" hesitated the girl who took it from her— "that he's to deliver it personally, Mamá?"

"Precisely." And without another word Josefa arose and left the room.

The sisters looked at one another uneasily. None of them found this errand to her liking. But there was nothing to be done. Someone was stuck with the job of infuriating Miguel. Perhaps it was Concepción who accepted the unpleasant duty. Or it may have been the unselfish, wide-eyed Luz, who looked so much like him. Whoever it was met the expected reaction.

"So I'm to hustle along to the rector with, of all things, an altar ornament?" he snorted. "Am I the priest's servant—or what?" he demanded, staring at the little parcel with distaste.

"For goodness' sake, Miguel, what's the matter with you? Mamá is going to hear you."

"All right, all right," he snapped, "I'll do it, but, believe me, only because it's her order."

Upon reaching the rectory, he was surprised out of his sulks to find there some long-time Jesuit friends of the Pros, Fathers Gordoa, Pautard, and Martínez. They were on their way to the Hacienda San Tiburcio to conduct a mission. They invited Miguel to go along with them. Though he certainly couldn't have said why, he found the idea very attractive.

In a rush of high spirits he returned to the house with the Jesuits to ask his father's permission to accompany them. And as soon as he had it, he burst in upon the family to amaze one and all with his jubilant: "I'm taking a vacation with the padres!" But what moved them almost to tears was when, dashingly clad in a vaquero (Mexican cowboy) outfit and astride a high-stepping mare, he cried with all the old gusto: "Adiós, adiós! I'm off to the good Fathers' mission!"

Josefa's happiness over her son's return to himself was boundless, but she still did not know what had been the matter with Miguel. She was to learn that only too soon. The first envelope to arrive from San Tiburcio, though addressed to her, contained a note he had written to a Protestant girl known to the family only by sight. The letter revealed that she and Miguel had been considering themselves engaged.

Josefa's pain at this discovery was soon somewhat softened by the other side of the embarrassing, but most fortunate, accident. This was that the young lady in question received in her envelope the letter meant for Josefa. In it a truly repentant son described the opening day of the mission. It had so touched his heart that he had confessed and received Communion. And his return to the sacraments had flooded his spirit with peace and gratitude. He was now begging his mother's pardon for his recent indifference and all the other offenses that had come of his inner confusion.

A most indignant señorita forwarded this letter to Doña Josefa, along with Miguel's earlier notes and presents to herself. For the mother there was, of course, great consolation in his change of heart. Just the same, the knowledge that there could have been any such deception under her own roof made her fall ill. She returned both letters to the hacienda—

not to her son but to Father Martinez. She was leaving it to him to tell the boy what had happened.

Following the discovery of his error, Miguel spent a whole night on his knees in the sanctuary. He blamed himself bitterly for having made his loved mother suffer by his stupid folly. For, as he had suspected from the beginning, it was no real affection that had gotten him romantically entangled with this girl. It was that, having declared himself in a rash moment, he had simply been too inexperienced to know how to get out of it. It had been his irritation with his foolishness and deceit that had turned him into a rebellious son and quarrelsome brother. Now, though terribly ashamed, he was thankful. For he knew that it had taken this disgrace to guide him out of an impossible situation.

Father Martínez wrote Josefa that Miguel's relief at having made his peace with heaven, his conscience, and his mother had sent his spirits soaring again. In fact, they had exploded in another prank, this time played on the padres.

Having dressed himself up in one of their stealthily borrowed soutanes, he had set out on a little preaching tour of his own about the neighboring ranchos. And what a success he had enjoyed with the simple countryfolk! They had listened reverently to the young "missionary's" sermons, kissed his hand, and filled his pockets with eggs, cheeses, even cigarettes —that is, until the real priests had caught up with him. But as this frisky Miguel had apparently done a fair job of the preaching, the Jesuits had contented themselves with carrying him back to the hacienda and relieving him of his collections.

Nor was the home-coming too hard. Josefa's understanding of her son's temperament smoothed his path back to happiness with the whole family.

3

Farewell to the Mines

BEFORE Miguel's eighteenth birthday, he was left in full charge of the agency while his father attended an engineers' convention at Zacatecas. Concepción had gone with Don Miguel because he wished her to know historic little Guadalupe, where she, Luz, and Miguel had been born. He would also be proud to show off his eldest child to the Pros' relatives and friends still living in this Zacatecas suburb. All these were so charmed by the gentle girl that, when it came time for Don Miguel to go, they begged him to leave her behind for a longer visit. Not only did he consent, but, upon his arrival home, he called Miguel and Luz aside to present them with their own tickets to Guadalupe.

"Wow!" exclaimed Miguel. "Does this really mean that . . . ?"

"Yes, Miguel, that I want you both to share your sister's holiday and to know the town of your birth as well as the sort of people I'm sorry you've been so long cheated of knowing. Afterward you can all come home together."

Luz was as overjoyed as Miguel at the prospect of seeing places they had heard so much about and, after their isolated years at the mines, associating with other young folk. Their father's "You'll be staying at the home of my good friend Don Luis Flores" had also suggested a program of exciting visits and expeditions.

Nor were they disappointed. Warmly welcomed by the Flores family, they were showered with invitations to all Guadalupe's best homes. For the first time in their memory, they were part of a circle of gay youngsters.

Almost the first place they were taken to see was Guadalupe's famed old Franciscan monastery where their distinguished great-uncle, Fray Juan Crisóstomo Gómez, lay buried. It was he who had given his favorite niece, their mother, the holy water with which they had all been baptized in this monastery's chapel. Here, too, they prayed beside the body of her girlhood confessor, Padre Galván, which lay in the crypt below the stairs that led to the archives.

To think that these records dated from the days of that great missionary to America's Indians, Venerable Antonio Margil de Jesús! Miguel became so interested in the register of miracles granted through the generations of holy men stationed at, or visiting, this apostolic college that he lost all sense of time.

When his sisters had finally coaxed Miguel away from the archives, he abruptly asked: "Do you know what I'd like best? No? Well, I'll tell you. To be one of these saints who eat, sleep, enjoy their little frolics and then—work miracles."

But just a few days later he was promising to fight a bull at the Violeta Club's annual fiesta. When they heard about this, Concepción and Luz were aghast. "And what do you know about bullfighting, for goodness' sake?" demanded

Concepción. "You must be crazy."

"You're bound to get hurt, and then what will Papá and Mamá have to say to us for permitting such a thing?" shuddered Luz.

"Well, but look, all the fellows are going to do it. Amateur fights are very much the thing around here. So I don't see how they can be so dangerous. Anyway, I can't back out now. Do you want all Guadalupe to think me a coward?"

But the girls weren't impressed. "We prohibit your doing it," said one. And the other added: "If you disobey us in this, you'll not find Our Lord helping you."

Reluctantly, he gave in. Though he would rather face any number of bulls than the scorn of his new friends, he didn't question that his older sisters represented authority in the absence of his parents.

A brilliant sun had risen upon the eagerly-awaited day. Now it was turning the toreador costumes into a riot of almost blinding colors. The whole town was out to admire the toreadors and otherwise enjoy the celebration. And so, though Miguel longed to avoid the whole thing, and especially the bullfight, it couldn't be done. Calling upon all his courage, he went along to the park to face his ordeal. The moment he was seen out of costume, eyebrows lifted, and the questions began.

"No, I'm not fighting," he explained over and over, "because my sisters have prohibited it, which, since they are older than I, it was their right to do." Just as he had expected, he was cruelly ridiculed, especially in the billiard parlor (which he forced himself to enter). How touching—not to say convenient—was such little brotherly obedience. And those pretty sisters—who would have dreamed them to be the older? But what a clever out for one who had regretted

his promise to take on a bull. To keep from striking the most insulting of his tormentors, Miguel had to cling desperately to a table with both hands.

But no one could force him to change his mind. In the afternoon, still giving no sign of his inner hurt, he took his sisters to the bull ring. There the very first thing that happened was that the Flores boy nearest his own age was savagely gored by the beast Miguel had been booked to fight as the opening event.

During the bullfight the Flores boy was savagely gored.

Leaving the girls in the care of friends, Miguel hurried to their host's injured son. The wound was critical and called for on-the-spot surgery. But now it was learned that the unlucky boy had a weak heart. The surgeon couldn't risk an anesthetic. Miguel offered to hold the poor chap through the operation. This was so excruciatingly painful, that young Flores at one point sank his teeth into Miguel's arm, biting a fair-sized piece of flesh out of it. Thus, at the conclusion of the operation, the doctor had to treat Miguel, too.

He spent the rest of the day at his friend's bedside, doubtless appreciating his sisters' wisdom in opposing his own absurd daring in agreeing to fight a bull.

Their vacation lasted three months, but there was always too much going on for Miguel's attention to return to the saints who had so fascinated him on that first visit to the monastery. Parties, picnics, and games were the order of the days. And meanwhile, Miguel, who had never paid much attention to his clothes, had become a fashion plate. To the girls' dismay, he had even used for his wardrobe the funds their father had twice forwarded for their return tickets.

Finally Don Miguel's patience ran out. He wrote Don Luis that his children must return to Concepción del Oro without further delay. Whereupon, Miguel accepted his father's order cheerfully.

It was only as he was handing the girls off the rickety train at the mine station that his heart sank into his shiny new boots. He had forgotten how really forlorn was the ragged community in which he had grown up. After Guadalupe's mellow charm, he saw the raw, straggling streets and ugly huddle of buildings before him as almost hideous. For a moment he was utterly discouraged that he might actually have to call such a graceless place home—forever. But then, in one of those characteristic quick lifts of the spirit, he smiled. "It's in God's hands," he startled the girls by stating.

Don Miguel had a special reason for calling them home. He was sending the family back to Saltillo for the little boys' schooling. Miguel, who must again become man of the house, saw a bit shamefacedly that his dread of having to settle down to the life of the mines had been unnecessary. Moreover, this time they were to occupy a house in one of

Saltillo's most desirable sections and right next door to the Jesuit College of San Juan Nepocumeno.

The life they took up there was as much more enjoyable as were their surroundings. Doña Josefa and her children were at once given cordial welcome into a society whose chief entertainments consisted of fiestas of the simpler sort, home musicales, and reading recitals. All of these gave the young Pros a wider audience for their own considerable talents.

Not long after their establishment in Saltillo in 1910 came the appearance of the famed Halley's comet. Alerted by the advance notices, Miguel excitedly posted himself to watch for the phenomenon. The instant he spotted its fiery trail against the rich night skies, he boisterously awakened the family. One and all must accompany him up a nearby hill where he would give them a class in astronomy. However, insistent though he was, only the girls and a half-awake Edmundo accepted his invitation.

Their brother's boundless enthusiasm over this wonder hadn't been satisfied by merely waking up everyone in his own household. Noisily caroling his liveliest songs as they passed through the streets, he managed to rouse the entire neighborhood.

At three o'clock when the comet reached perfect visibility, his exclamation was one of awe and wonder. "Viva! My heavenly Father, the Worker of such perfection!" Another change of mood and he was suddenly crying: "Just wait, all you little—or big— stars, until you see how I shall outdo you in blazing my track across the heavens! Isn't that right, boys?" he challenged. "Yes, yes, yes, yes!"

On the fourth "yes," a night watchman descended upon the noise-maker with a demand for quiet. But this only drew the loudest shout yet from Miguel. "My good man, just look at what's above your head and see if you can speak of quiet. Isn't that right, boys? Yes, yes, yes!"

"Silence!" implored the harassed watchman. "Do you want to wake up the whole city?"

"I think I do," came the airy reply. "And why shouldn't we want to share our rejoicing with everybody, eh?" Whereupon he flung his hat into the air and burst into song again.

Since carting a group of well-born young people off to jail was unthinkable, the poor watchman had to accept defeat for the moment. The next morning, however, he lodged a complaint with Doña Josefa. During the interview, Miguel, standing in seeming sorrow on the sidelines, was actually plotting his revenge. At the height of the discussion, he managed, unseen, to attach a long cord to the man's lantern. Then, clutching the cord's free end, he slipped out of the room. The watchman caught a flash of his light sliding from sight around the door frame and forthwith broke off his warning in the middle of a sentence to give chase. Down the street flew Miguel, the lantern, and the watchman—whose embarrassment wasn't lessened by the laughter of everyone they passed.

And so both pleasant and enlivening were these second two years in Saltillo. But at least one of the children realized that this easygoing existence must end and they must soon embark on their own individual lives. To the others, though, Luz's announcement that she was leaving for Aguascalientes to become a nun came as a real surprise. A surprise? To Miguel the news that he was losing Luz, his orchestra's very best musician, was the greatest and sorest shock he had ever known. How was it possible for her to disrupt their good life and so cheerfully at that? He could barely bring himself to congratulate her.

4

The Decision

MIGUEL told himself that Luz's desertion had spoiled everything. Not only did he sadly miss his sister, her going had very pointedly shown up the fact that here *he* was, at nineteen and a half, still without any plan for his own future.

"What's the matter with me that this girl has beaten me so badly in finding her way?" he demanded of Concepción.

It was a nagging thought he couldn't even forget in his music, since Luz's absence had left such a maddening hole in the orchestra. He tried to hide his bitterness from his parents so as not to deepen their loneliness for her. But Concepción, following a concert particularly displeasing to him, heard his muttered: "Caramba! How great heaven must be if it's got to be bought at such a price."

Six months later, just as he had begun to grow used to their loss, came the invitation to Luz's reception of the habit. Since this was the biggest event so far in the lives of the Pro children, it must be witnessed by them all. So the whole family traveled to Aguascalientes for the beautiful ceremony and some visiting.

A few days later, leaving the others to enjoy the sightseeing, Concepción and Josefa set out on a mysterious side trip to León that left Miguel plagued by a terrible worry. He realized that the motherhouse of the Order Luz had joined was in León. All too soon he learned that Concepción, too, would disappear forever from the world they had so enjoyed together.

After the first shock, he asked Concepción to take a last walk with him. And when they were alone he begged her to tell him what it was that could cause her to enter the convent and abandon her loved ones in such an abrupt fashion.

"The will of God," she told him gently.

"Well, then, there's nothing to do," he sadly replied. "But what, I ask you, is His will for me? Do pray to Him to tell me, and soon, sister."

The next morning little brother Humberto made his First Communion. Luz, who had been his godmother at Baptism, was his sponsor this time, too. (Having a sponsor at First Communion is the custom in Mexico.) At the breakfast, the Pros' last all together, Miguel suddenly demanded of his two sisters who had pledged themselves to religion: "Why shouldn't *I* do the same thing?"

Their only answer was a shared smile. Whereupon, the words tumbling from his full heart, he added: "If what I'm feeling this minute is a divine call, that's how it's going to turn out." It was the first time in his twenty years that Miguel

Agustín Pro had ever admitted the possibility of his own vocation.

That same day Concepción accompanied her sister back to the convent, and the others prepared to return to Saltillo. Again Miguel was sunk in deepest discouragement, nor did getting home and the passing of the months lighten his mood.

Doña Josefa wrote her convent daughters that they really wouldn't know Miguel. Their gay, prankplaying brother had become most disturbingly reserved and thoughtful. Trying as his old practical jokes had sometimes been, how greatly she would now welcome their return. It broke her heart to see him always so sober, so silent. Lately, too, he had taken to disappearing for several hours at a stretch. And from wherever it was that he went, he returned to head straight for his room which he then paced for hours to and fro. There was surely something very wrong with Miguel. His sisters must pray for him—and hard.

It had been most sobering for Miguel finally to recognize what it was that God wanted of him: that he exchange his useless existence for total dedication to his fellow men. In short, that he become a priest. For though it was a blessing to see his future at long last settled, he couldn't be very gay about it until he had found a way to achieve it. This promised to be a lot more difficult than he had imagined. Right off he had learned how mistaken he had been in expecting the next-door Jesuits to receive him with open arms. Rather, Padre Gabriel Morfín, Rector of San Juan Nepocumeno College, had given him so altogether shabby a dismissal that Miguel was certain his old friends and neighbors must be heartily laughing at his efforts to join that brilliant company.

Trying to rest his aching bones, Miguel was lying on his

bed, turning hot, then cold, as he relived that awful afternoon which had begun with his tapping on the Father Rector's study door, right on time for his appointment. How eagerly he had obeyed the answering "Come in." Even while crossing the threshold, he was greeting Father Morfín with the most respectful phrases at his command.

And what had happened? Exactly nothing. Because the priest, whom he found settled deeply in a rocking chair, reading a newspaper, hadn't so much as looked up at his entrance. Without offering Miguel the courtesy of a seat or in any other way taking the least notice of his presence, he had gone right on reading the paper. Before such a strange—wasn't it deliberately insulting?—reception, Miguel had felt his face blazing with embarrassment. What in the world was he supposed to do? he was asking himself as he shifted uncomfortably from one foot to the other. Could there have been a misunderstanding about the appointment? Even so, how could the man just sit there rudely ignoring a caller he had in any case bidden to enter the room? From his first surprise and dismay, Miguel's resentment had soon risen to such a pitch that he felt like tipping the complacent rector right out of his rocker.

Nevertheless, he could be stubborn, too; and so, for a full half-hour, he had doggedly stood there, not once taking his eyes from the rector's face. His whole body was hurting from the strain when, at length, the Jesuit did glance up. But this was only to suggest offhandedly: "You'd best come back tomorrow, my son, since, as you see, I'm exceedingly busy today."

It seemed almost unbelievable that he had managed to say, "Very well, Father, and good afternoon," without choking on his fury.

Miguel was left standing in the room as Padre Morfín wrote on.

Back home again, it had been almost more than he could do to keep from telling his mother how outrageously he had been treated by one of those "excellent and holy men" next door. But, he kept silent because he didn't want her to know about his decision to become a priest until he could also say that someone in authority had given him encouragement.

For a long time, or until exhaustion had dropped him upon the bed, he had paced this room, arguing with himself about ever going back to see Padre Morfín. On the one hand, he told himself that this worst humiliation of his life must have been the rector's way of getting rid of him. On the other, mightn't the rudeness have really been unintentional?

In the end, Miguel pocketed his pride and returned to the college the next day. But his second try at talking to the rector was just as unsuccessful. This time he found Padre Morfín writing what appeared to be an endless document. Once again, and for a much longer time than on the day before, poor Miguel was left standing in the middle of the room, grinding his teeth with rage. Hardly able to breathe without spluttering, he squirmed, stared at the rector, and promised himself that if he didn't look up within five minutes to ask: "What may I do for you, my son?" Miguel Pro would never be idiot enough to set foot on these premises again.

And then? Well, when Padre Morfín finally signed whatever it was he had been writing and pushed back his chair, it was to say: "See here, young man, as I'm even busier today than I was yesterday, you'll have to return another time. How would tomorrow afternoon suit you?"

Miguel would never know how he managed to hold his tongue while he stalked out of the door. But in the patio he promptly ran into another situation so astounding that he almost forgot his grievance. For there he found several of the younger religious openly, in fact loudly, complaining of their lot in life. Who else had to suffer as many trials and hardships as they who had given up everything to join this Order?

He could hardly believe his ears. That men of God could carry on like this, especially in the hearing of a young layman . . . But when some of them broke off their grumbling to start teasing him on his visits to the college, the light suddenly came. Why, of course, Padre Morfín and these Fathers as well had been testing his patience and perseverance. If he were the discourageable type, they intended to discourage him ahead of time.

In a flash, Miguel's misery was a thing of the past. For now that he had seen through their little plot, he would pit his own talent for play-acting against theirs. From that moment, he undertook this with such energy and good will that he had soon convinced Padre Morfín and everyone else that he was possessed of the long-suffering, persistence, and humor so necessary to a successful priest.

Still Miguel delayed telling his parents. And though by now they must have guessed where all these hours spent at the college were leading, they never spoke of them to him. Even when he one day hinted: "I've got a little piece of business on with the Jesuit padres," they apparently made nothing of it.

Finally they learned for certain that their son had been accepted by the Order when he suddenly fell seriously ill. For during his delirium, Miguel ceaselessly chattered about his triumph and even revealed the hiding place of his letters from the Jesuits' Mexican Provincial, Padre Ipiña. These proved that he had been accepted by the Society.

Once he was well again, he explained everything and then said, "So with your permission, dear Papá and Mamá, I'm going to leave you to enter the service of Jesus Christ."

By now quite convinced of his vocation, they gave him their blessings. "There's just one thing I must insist upon," said Don Miguel. "It's that I accompany you to the Michoacán novitiate where they're sending you. You've been too sick too recently to make a long trip alone."

"But I'm fine now, Papá, really."

"Very well, son. Let's just say, then, that your father covets the honor of personally delivering you into the hands of the Almighty Father."

It was on August 10, 1911, that Miguel and his father reached Hacienda El Llano, the novitiate. Don Miguel stayed over until Assumption Day to see his son's clothing in the habit. Then, after Mass, the wise and generous father embraced Miguel once more and, leaving him to start his new life, turned his face homeward alone.

5

Troubled Novitiate

A FEW months earlier, the government under which Miguel had lived his whole life had finally been overthrown. From one day to the next, Mexico's so-called "Iron Man," the dictator Porfirio Díaz, had been ousted by Francisco Madero's revolution. And because Madero had promised the nation some overdue reforms, the majority of Mexicans welcomed the change. Because of his deep sympathy for the poor, Miguel had been thankful to be entering religion at what seemed so hopeful a time in his country's history.

So far all his efforts had gone into making himself acceptable to the Society of Jesus, but now he was almost frightened to realize how much study lay before him. Sometimes he wondered how he, a fellow already past twenty who hadn't even finished high school, had dared seek a place in a society of men world-famed for their learning.

But he knew any victory could be won by sufficient prayer. So, while studying hard, he prayed even more. Very soon his classmates and professors were calling him "the brother who is so sure God wants him to be a saint."

But Miguel never lost his love of the little joke, the clever take-off, or just simple play. His good humor made him popular with his brother-novices; his wittiness and theatrical knowledge made him the star of their plays and literary events.

In fact, as Padre Adolfo Pulido, perhaps the closest of his seminary friends, tells us: ". . . there were two Pros, the one who played and the one who prayed; the one who joked, laughed and sang, and the one of abnegation and silence. ... Of us all it was he who spent the most time on his knees before the Blessed Sacrament."

Certainly there were plenty of trials for him to pray himself through. One of them arose from his assignment to the post of messenger. After having delivered the superiors' instructions to the students satisfactorily for more than a month, he made his first slip. Novice Master Father Santiago saw fit to use this to test his attitude toward authority. Visiting Miguel's cell, he bawled him out and fired him as messenger, punishments more severe than his mistake called for. Afterward, Father Santiago fairly stamped out of the room in what seemed to be great indignation.

Nevertheless, a half-hour later, Miguel was knocking on his door. "I've come to beg your pardon, Father, for this failure in my duty," he said, with the sincerest humility. Poor

Father Santiago was almost undone by the success of his experiment.

Even so, he made the next test still harder. For in addition to all the seminarians and teachers, it took place before the bishop himself. Father Santiago was well aware of Miguel's reputation as a comic storyteller. So on the occasion of the bishop's first visit to El Llano, he suddenly ordered his novice: "Go ahead, Brother Pro, and tell His Excellency some of your funny stories. I'm sure he will find them most amusing."

Miguel was aghast. What in the world would the bishop think of a would-be Jesuit given to rattling off such stupid nonsense? But obedience was obedience. So, though fiery-faced with shame, he began: "Well, you see, Your Excellency, there was this old billy goat . . ." Somehow he got through one of his silliest yarns. The seminarians never forgot this painful scene.

But his humility and obedience would be fully rewarded. His superiors, completely satisfied, on August 15, 1913, permitted Miguel Agustín Pro to take the vows that made him a member of the great Society of Jesus.

Before this important milestone had been reached at peaceful El Llano, great sections of Mexico had been plunged into frightful violence. Madero had been unable to control the firebrands his revolution had loosed upon the country, and a whole series of new, independent revolts had broken out. Worse still, they were led by men who hated religion. Whatever their differences and competing ambitions, they were one in their determination to root it out of "Revolutionary Mexico."

Needless to say, the Church's properties would also come in very handy for the financing of their campaigns and political notions. And if those despised priests couldn't be tortured into handing over the large sums that were going to be demanded of them, why, it would be a pleasure to throw them to the firing squads.

However, until the trouble already engulfing the north reached Michoacán, the El Llano superiors believed it their duty to remain at their posts where they were forming men of peace. Thus, for nearly a year following his profession, Miguel went on without any interruption in his studies. And though he wasn't a brilliant scholar, especially of Latin and Greek, he did shine as a writer of both prose and poetry. And his talent for public speaking promised to make him a powerful preacher.

But day by day the terror was drawing closer as, one after another, the cities fell before the onslaughts of Pancho Villa, Venustiano Carranza, and Álvaro Obregón. After hearing about the torture of the priests of the College of San Juan Nepocumeno when Saltillo was taken by Villa, the seminary fathers began preparing for the dispersion. Quickly but quietly they arranged for their students to be distributed among the trusted families in the vicinity. Secular clothing was obtained, a suit or two at a time, in nearby Zamora. The best monastery books, pictures, images, and altar ornaments were either placed in the hands of the faithful or buried under the floor of the seminary carpenter shop.

It was none too soon. By the first of August, Zamora had fallen to the followers of Carranza, the Carrancistas. And at one o'clock on the morning of the fifth, El Llano received its warning. A raiding party of twenty-two, bristling with firearms, galloped up to the hacienda's gatehouse.

"Open up and make it snappy!" snarled the leader to the watchman. And when he had, the party, discharging their pistols right and left, clattered up to the absent owner's residence. Hacking down the barred doors, they chopped his furniture to bits, burned his account books, cut his telephone line, and destroyed whatever else they could find.

With the first shots, the seminary rector and another Jesuit stationed themselves at the chapel door, prepared to give their lives to protect the sacred objects. Fortunately, however, on this occasion the vandals did not attack the church. But the next morning Miguel found some of their bullets in the chapel wall.

It was nightfall on August 12,1914, that the rector gathered his students together to give them the sad word. They must leave their monastery to face their immediate futures on their own. "Your superiors will strive to keep in touch with you and may soon be able to send you on to the Society's novitiates in other countries. Meanwhile, we must all pray to God for our eventual reunion."

The next morning, by twos and threes, they slipped out of El Llano, bound for homes in Zamora or its neighboring haciendas. Even though the clergy was now being persecuted as furiously here as anywhere else in the country, it was hoped that the seminarians might not be recognized as such. Most of them were from other sections, and the townspeople weren't familiar with their faces.

Miguel and his companion arrived in due course at their Zamora address to be warmly welcomed by a fine family. But instead of staying under cover, the very next day they volunteered for the risky job of carrying food to a pair of local priests who were hiding out in the hills.

"We'll be all right," Miguel cheerfully assured their worried hostess. "We're not known in Zamora. Aren't we your visiting nephews? And can't we go hiking if we like?"

For the first few days everything went off on schedule.

Rucksacks on mountain climbers didn't look suspicious. If their gear were examined, the seminarians could say the food was for themselves. In any case, they weren't challenged. Nor was anyone about when they reached the place agreed upon for hiding the food, which would be picked up by the padres after their departure.

But then came the night when their return was so delayed that the household was sure they had been caught.

"We're awfully sorry," explained Miguel when they finally did get back, "but we couldn't help it; that is, if we were going to follow the Señora's advice about being careful. You see, we'd no sooner hidden the fathers' dinner than we heard horses, dozens of them, galloping toward us. Knowing they had to be Carrancistas, we ducked into a full-grown cornfield. And there, hardly breathing, we squatted for an hour or more while these fellows rode up and down examining the whole location. They'd certainly been tipped off that something was going on around there.

"Though we were plenty scared, at the same time we had to laugh at their stupidity. Can you imagine a searching party investigating every tree and boulder and simply not noticing a cornfield high enough to cover an army? Anyway, even after they'd given it up and gone on, we weren't anxious to leave that blessed corn. And that's why we're so late."

The next day came the instructions from their superiors. All seminarians without families in Zamora were to leave the town in groups immediately for various destinations. Miguel and three others must get to the town of Negrete by whatever means they could, and there catch a train for Guadalajara.

"But how in the world do they expect you to get by the guards posted at all the exits?" exclaimed their hostess. "Don't they know nobody's allowed to leave the city without a passport personally signed by this villainous Carrancista commander?"

"I think it's going to be rather fun," said Miguel—and he meant it. For this was just the sort of dare to appeal to his actor's instinct. And he had already selected the role of peasant, the one most likely to see him safely past the outposts.

Fortunately it was a cold, wet August evening, reason enough for the innocent-looking peasant to have his serape pulled up to the nose, his sombrero down to the eyes. His pajama legs were just sufficiently mud-splattered. And as he shuffled along the cobblestones toward the open country, his huaraches showed feet just the right Indian brown. If anyone jerked aside the serape, his face and hands would be seen to match exactly. And, of course, his eyes were naturally as dark as any Indian's. The shuffle, posture, the mannerisms were equally typical. Nevertheless, it was with every sense alerted that he approached the danger point, a lean-to under which several uniformed figures were huddled about a smoldering fire.

And then he had to hold back a hearty laugh. The only sense he had needed was his hearing. Because, to the last man of them, the guards were lustily snoring. Almost sorry his make-up and acting ability weren't going to be put to the test, he drifted right by them without being seen.

Just the same, he was mighty thankful for the serape and sombrero during the long night he spent in the open fields awaiting the arrival of the rest of his group. Even so, as the rain became an August deluge, he was soaked to the skin before the fourth member of the party showed up at daybreak.

It was a bedraggled, shivering little company that set out, after a sleepless night, on the killingly long and hazardous

For hours the seminarians remained motionless in the cornfield.

tramp to Negrete. The going could scarcely have been tougher. The so-called roads were ankle-deep in mud. Slogging and skidding ahead, they dared not relax their lookout for armed parties for a single instant. Their watch was made much harder by the blinding downpour, but they could not hope, at this season, for any slackening of the rain.

"What's coming over that hill?" demanded one of them on the second morning of their march, as he pointed into the distance directly ahead.

"I should say," replied Miguel with a little grimace, "that it's our exit cue—into this nice thick growth of bushes and brambles. For it can't be less than a full platoon of Carrancistas."

Without another word, they all plunged into the undergrowth to wait until the soldiers either had passed them by or discovered them. But it wasn't going to be that easy. "Chihuahua," whispered Miguel after a cautious peek at the force which was now within a hundred yards of them, "they're halting."

As indeed they were—to build fires, fling up shelters, eat, and take what seemed to the seminarians an endless siesta. For hours the seminarians were condemned to remain motionless, but sinking ever deeper into the mud, with water running in rivers through their clothing. It was late afternoon before their blue-lipped prayers were answered as the troop remounted and rode on past them—so closely that the horses whipped the brambles into their faces. Half-paralyzed, the four crawled out of the bushes to stumble on toward Negrete.

Miguel was the only one of them pretending to be a peasant. When they finally boarded the train, he acted as the others' servant. At first his juggling of their skimpy luggage and jumping to wait on them hand and foot gave them all they could do to keep from laughing. But soon they were actually forgetting he wasn't the genuine article under his enormous sombrero and serape.

Pancho Villa's victory at Saltillo had also bitterly affected the whole Pro family. To begin with, it had forced Don Miguel, a known federal employee, to flee for his life, leaving his family unprotected. And the reason Miguel had been sent to Guadalajara was that, after Pancho Villa's men had seized all the Pros' possessions, that was where Doña Josefa had taken her three younger sons and Ana María. He had expected to find them in poor circumstances, but never suspected that it could be as bad as this.

Delighted as he was by their reunion, it broke his heart to see his mother, accustomed to a comfortable, well-supplied house, struggling to maintain her children in one wretched boardinghouse room, containing but two beds and some chairs. But this wonderful woman had not lost hope because she had not lost faith.

Since he could now so well appreciate her perfect acceptance of God's will, the usually talkative Miguel didn't dare mention how badly he felt over his inability to help. His vows had been taken, a glorious fact he wouldn't have changed. But knowing he must soon leave them penniless in such a place was the heaviest cross he had ever borne.

Nevertheless, he romped and joked with his little brothers, speaking only to God about his worries over their future. The grief that must not escape in words found other ways of making itself felt. He was attacked by almost continuous headaches, and there was something very wrong with his stomach. But these pains, too, he hid from Josefa. Her joy in these few weeks mustn't be spoiled. Between the necessary meetings with his brother-seminarians, he gave her all the companionship he could.

He had to get together daily with his fellow escapees from Zamora for their religious observances. After September 12, when Obregón's men closed the churches, it was difficult just to hear Mass. Hunting out this and then that residence where it was being illegally celebrated, the seminarians had to make sure not to be seen too often in the same neighborhood or too often together. The revolutionists' spies were everywhere. And if they discovered these Masses, they would take over the houses in which they were said and cart their loyal owners, along with the priests, off to jail—or worse.

So the mornings were exciting all right. And afterward, the young Jesuits would re-gather in some safe place for their devotions, to discuss their situation, and guess about the future.

Then things got better for the seminarians scattered all over the city. One of their El Llano priests arrived to guide them. This solved the problems of Mass attendance, Communion, visits to the Blessed Sacrament. And very soon came the word that, the railway being more or less repaired, they would leave at once for the United States. Miguel and six others would be the first to depart.

"Well, Mamá, it's another good-by," he said, as he stood with his arm about Josefa's frail shoulders on the sooty station platform. He kept his voice very firm so she wouldn't see how much more than usual this good-by was affecting him. And she who had always wept at their partings merely smiled calmly up at him. Minutes later, from the last mud-splattered old coach, Miguel was waving to the little knot of Pros on the platform. . . .

It was a ghastly journey. The train was filthy and so old and worn out that every few miles it broke down. The rest of the time it just crawled through a desert that would have been desolate enough before the fighting. Now it was dotted with overturned, rusting trains, the blackened ruins of burned stations, shot-up and burned-out ghost towns and shattered bridges.

"Welcome to the United States," called out the Jesuit who met them at Laredo, Texas. His broad smile was in warm contrast to the suspicious official scowls they had been given just over the line. And they were made welcome just as warmly by all the North American religious they met. At San Antonio, it was the Oblates who opened their house to these young refugees and saw to it that they rested from their tiring trip. A few days later their kindly hosts were their own El Paso Jesuits with whom, to their joy, they could speak Spanish. But this, too, was just a short break in their westward way.

The fathers at Los Gatos, California, where Miguel's group arrived on October 9, 1914, received them and all those who followed them with open arms. They gladly overcrowded their seminary by turning two of its buildings over to the Mexicans. What they couldn't provide were Spanish textbooks, and the priest-professors who escaped the revolutionaries to join them hadn't been able to bring any along.

If Miguel fretted over his failure to progress in their bookless classes and the continued bad news from his family, and if he was now suffering almost constant stomach pains, none of this showed in his cheerful, jolly manner. His good humor and fine wit made him many friends among the Los Gatos Jesuits.

But the California stay wasn't to be long. That same year

came the instructions that sent Miguel across a vast continent and a still vaster sea to Spain where most of his long exile would be spent. He was not sorry.

"If we can't go home," he kept telling those who went with him, "we couldn't ask for a lovelier place to live and study than Spain's beautiful Granada."

6

The Teacher

"**B**UT where *is* everyone?" demanded the stranger. "What's going on that the stores and houses are all closed up tighter than drums?"

"Why," replied the only soul he had been able to find on the main street of little Lanjarón, Spain, "this is Catechism Day. So naturally, they're all over in the woods with Padrecito Miguel." (For this was what the peasants of the broad Granadina Plain called Miguel Pro long before his ordination.) "It's always the same at Huétor Santillán, Albolote, any of the towns round about. The Padrecito catches most everybody with his catechism class, brings 'em in from all the farms, too—men, women, and children."

It was true. After five years of hard study at Granada, where he had made no outstanding record, Miguel had turned out to be his seminary's most famous and successful catechist. The people dropped everything to go hear this young Mexican give instructions on their Faith in their own dialect. The homely humor with which he spiced his lessons gave them many hearty laughs and helped to attract his unheard-of audience.

For the rest, his kindness and humor kept him a favorite with his classmates, very few of whom suspected that when he was the gayest he was covering his worst moments. Had there just been a letter from home reporting Don Miguel's continuing absence and silence? Were his stomach pains more violent than usual? Or was he bearing both these miseries together? Such were the times that he always managed to tell the most and funniest stories, to sing the most rollicking songs. Then, too, he would ask to wait on the table or perform some other yet more menial service. But all his patience and humility were being rewarded in the success of his catechizing.

So it was hard to hear his superior say: "Brother Pro, you're off to another Granada. You'll spend the two years our students always teach before beginning their Theology at the school our exiled Mexicans have opened in Granada, Nicaragua."

"Very good, Father," smiled Miguel. "And may I know what class I'm to take?"

"Oh, you've no cause for worry," teased the superior. "You are being assigned to the first grade." It was hard to be going back across the great ocean without a hope of entering his own beloved country, where the religious persecution was now more terrible than ever, or seeing his dear family. But by now Miguel Pro was able to take true happiness in the hardships. And anyway, he always made himself dwell upon the optimistic side of everything.

There were five years of hard study at Granada.

"How much I'll like working under my own Mexican fathers again," he enthused to his companions.

But once in Nicaragua what couldn't have been very enjoyable were the multitudes of poisonous insects and snakes produced by its hot and humid climate. Through the open window-frames giving onto a rank jungle growth, reptiles came crawling at all hours.

"Each night," Miguel wrote to his friends in Spain, "we have to examine the dormitory beds very carefully for snakes and scorpions, and then keep making the rounds all night long to recheck. Another of our excellent discouragers of laziness is the simply flooding rain at this season. I'm in charge of the little fellows' dormitory and I sleep, that is, supposedly, in an alcove just off it. But when it storms, I'm up and down all night to keep moving the beds from under the *bigger* leaks in the roof and to comfort those whom the crashing thunder and lightning terrorize."

"Our teacher is really something," one small Nicaraguan who couldn't go home for the vacations told his father on visitors' day. "When it gets just too hot for baseball or anything like that and we are homesick besides, he plays his guitar and sings funny songs for us. Or maybe he'll say, 'Let's do some charades.' He always knows new games, too, that we can play in the shade or indoors. All of us think he's the best teacher in the world!" No wonder that the little boys were fighting back the tears when they had to say good-by forever to their Brother Pro.

It was 1922 and he was thirty-one years old when he was ordered back to Sarria, Spain, to commence his Theology. There he would occasion no complaints of his scholarship. In Theology, Canon Law, and Sociology he made such fine grades that he was soon selected to go to the famed Jesuit

School of Theology at Enghien, Belgium.

Since the hundred men at Enghien came from thirteen nations, they had to speak Latin to one another. But because of the many accents—French, Spanish, English, German, and so on—there couldn't be very much natural conversation in this house. So it wasn't easy to make new friends. Sometimes Miguel wondered if any of the busy theologians even knew his name. But anyone who ever rapped on his door with a message or to ask a favor could be sure of a hearty welcome.

"Come in, Father, do come in. What a pleasure!" Thus, as everywhere, the whole house was soon aware of the Mexican's good nature and merry disposition.

The thing no one knew about was his always worsening pain which kept him awake almost all night and prevented him from eating anything to speak of for days at a time. But in spite of his weakened condition, he gladly accepted an invitation by the Americans to play baseball during recreation. And these contests he called: "Calles against Coolidge," using the names of the presidents of Mexico and the United States.

For now it was Plutarco Elías Calles who reigned by firing squad over luckless Mexico. Carranza, Villa, and others were dead—of the same sort of violence they had practiced. But not Álvaro Obregón, who had passed the power he had snatched from Carranza on to Calles for safekeeping. These two cynics, it now seemed, would be their nation's alternating dictators indefinitely. From his mother's letters, Miguel knew that the change certainly had not improved matters for their anything but liberated people. Rather they had altogether lost the basic human rights to profess and practice their Faith and to control the education of their children. Though Miguel hadn't given up hope of returning to minister to his own, the outlook for that was thus still very black.

He wrote Josefa that he was now preparing himself for "the apostolate to the workers." Having discovered the great papal encyclicals on labor, "I've dedicated myself to obtaining the wisdom to preach and teach this fascinating subject of social justice. How inspiring it is to know that the popes defined it all so clearly many years before our revolutionists opened their savage persecution in, and only in, its name!"

And now he was about to be ordained priest and start the great work. So awed was he by this tremendous approaching event that he could hardly persuade himself that he was going to be accepted. The sickness he had borne alone through all these long years of study may also have been partially responsible for his discouragement. He had even written his Nicaraguan confessor, Father Bernardo Portas, of his fears.

But when he wrote his next letter he was indeed in the clouds. "I send this to give you a little piece of news. I'm saying my first Mass on August 31. . . . Be happy with me and aid me with your sacrifices and prayers to give thanks to God for this supreme favor and to procure from Him my worthiness to receive such a priceless Sacrament.

"You'll doubtless want to send me a present, no? Because just see what a spiritual son heaven has given *you*. Well, don't think I shall oppose the gift. Far from it. Yes, send whatever you choose to (even if it be a letter), just as long as it isn't a scorpion, a papaya, or a banana. . . ."

On the last day of August, 1925, along with twenty others—eighteen French, a Brazilian, and an American—Miguel Agustín Pro was ordained a Jesuit priest by Monseigneur Le Comte. It was a real sorrow that, almost alone among this company, he was denied the joy of bestowing his first blessings upon his beloved family. But it wasn't an enduring sadness.

"At last we are priests," he was soon saying to one of his companions, "and that is enough."

There was another joy from which Padre Pro was excluded. Owing to his broken French, he couldn't preach. But he celebrated Mass in the local churches and convents. And very soon he had gotten permission for a visit to the Charleroi coal mines—to get acquainted with the Belgian miners, their working conditions, and problems. He felt sure this should help him prepare for his apostolate to the workers.

As he went down into Charleroi's deepest, darkest galleries with the miners and listened to their complaints, he seemed to be back again in Concepción del Oro. How alike were the frustrations of this world's laborers! And how many of these, as a result of their dissatisfactions, had turned away from Christ and His Church. Young Father Miguel was on fire to help them—spiritually by bringing them back to the Faith, materially by preaching their cause to the owners and lawmakers. And this went for all those other workers in the factories and foundries that he also investigated.

He took his place in the Catholic Worker Youth movement and attended their Social Study Week at Fayt-lez-Manage in September. He told its directors: "I want to arm myself with all your information, learn your technique for missionizing the laborers and underprivileged. It's my dearest hope to one day use everything you can teach me in favor of my own people."

One day Padre Miguel entered a third-class railway car to find before him ten miners who were on an excursion from Charleroi. He couldn't fail to notice their resentment at the addition of a foreign priest to their company. One or two grunts were all his friendly "Good afternoon" was able to produce. Whereafter, as he took his seat, the men all remained stonily and rudely silent.

But Miguel Pro had always been the talkative type, and now he set about breaking down this hostility by asking questions.

"Pardon me, sir, but what is the name of this station?" Silence.

"Is it a large town?" Silence.

"What is its industry?"

"Look, *Monsieur l'Abbé*, we are all socialists."

"Well, fine," responded the Father. "I'm a socialist, too."

Ten astonished faces swung to look at him. "*Monsieur l'Abbé* a socialist!" exclaimed the one who had spoken to him in the hope of offending.

"Yes, gentlemen, I'm a socialist, if not exactly your sort of socialist who doesn't know what socialism really is. Tell me, now, can one of you explain just what it is to be a socialist?"

After a moment's hesitation one of the other miners ventured, "It's to take all their money from the rich."

Father Pro scratched his head reflectively and then suggested, "Well, but that gives us a problem. For, when we've got all that money in our hands, what arrangements are we supposed to make to protect it from *thieves?*"

This drew some smiles, but, just the same, it wouldn't do to let this joker get away with anything.

"Some of us are really Communists."

"Communists, too, eh?" mused Father Pro. Then he flashed them a wide grin. "Good. I'm also a Communist. Look, it's already one o'clock and some of you are eating. That's fine, but I'm hungry, too. Wouldn't you like to divide your lunch with me?"

There was a general laugh at the man who had let himself into this trap. Annoyed, he demanded, "Weren't you afraid to come into our compartment?"

Father Pro appeared not to have heard correctly. "Afraid? Why—when I'm always well armed?"

"Perhaps you'd best show us your pistol, *Monsieur l'Abbé*, the socialist!" snapped the miner menacingly.

The priest at once began rummaging in his pockets until a smile of relief showed that he had located his "arms." The air was filled with tension. "Here is my weapon. With it along I fear no one." Then Padre Miguel displayed his crucifix to ten suddenly sheepish-looking faces. From there on to their destination, the miners let this unusual cleric hold the floor —which he did with a talk on the effective operation of his "weapon" that was so much more powerful than a pistol. How deeply his words struck home he couldn't know, but several of these Charleroi miners removed their hats as he continued to hold the crucifix before their eyes.

At Châtelineau, where the miners left the train, one of them shoved a small package into Padre Pro's hands. When he was alone in the carriage he opened it. It was filled with chocolate pastry.

Padre Pro could no longer hide his illness. His cheerful disposition was not affected, but pain and undernourishment had changed his physical appearance so distressingly that everyone around him noticed it. Finally his superior felt compelled to speak to him about it.

"You are very ill, aren't you, Father?"

"I have pain," admitted Padre Miguel, "but I think we can ignore it. You see, Your Reverence, it is now ten or more years old," he smiled apologetically, "but it hasn't yet disrupted my work. And I certainly don't want it to do so now, just when I'm starting both my Catholic Worker activities and my Theology IV."

"But surely it has been worsening of late?"

"I haven't been giving it much thought, Your Reverence."

"Well, your superiors have," came the stern reply. "And while your bravery is to be admired, something must be done. You are eating practically nothing, and I'm sure you don't need telling that the recent change in your physical appearance is quite shocking. So we must get your trouble diagnosed and under treatment without further delay."

"May I suggest that all this will take time, Reverend Father? There is so much I'd like to do before . . . Well, let's merely say the doctoring *could* be useless."

"Your superiors must be the judges of how your time is spent."

"Very well, Father, whatever you say!"

Thus there began for Miguel Pro the weary program of examinations, diets, medicines, and, finally, a six months' session in a sanitarium—right at the beginning of his ministry. But as he had dreaded, nothing came of so much attention save the discovery that his life depended upon an immediate operation.

It was left to his spiritual director, Father Bouvy, to tell him and gain his consent to the surgery. "This one more trial now, my son, may well mean your cure. At the least it should preserve you for some years of fruitful labors."

"I'm not afraid of physical suffering," answered the sick young priest.

"Well, then, we may consider it settled. And I'm sure you'll have reason to rejoice that you agreed to have the operation."

"It shall be whatever you think best, Father, and thank you," sighed Miguel, who wasn't especially encouraged by his counselor's optimism.

He was at once sent to the Saint-Rémi Clinic in Brussels

where he was to undergo not one, but three, operations. It was right after the first that he received the blow which made him forget his merely physical agony. Josefa, his wonderful mother, was dead. All his thirty-five years she had been closer to his heart than any other human being.

The moment Father Enrique Basabe heard of his friend's great loss, he hurried right over to the hospital to offer his sympathy. Miguel told him how it had been.

"I can't be sure whether my first reaction to the awful news was serenity or just stupefaction. Whatever it was, I couldn't shed a single tear. But later, at night when I was alone, I clasped my crucifix and wept quite desperately."

"And now?" smiled his visitor tenderly.

"I am greatly consoled. You see, I *know* what a holy death she died. Yes, I was never surer of anything than I am that she is already in heaven."

Before the second very complicated operation on his stomach, the surgeons had to tell him that this time they couldn't risk an anesthetic.

"That's all right," was his calm reply. "But then please be so good as to send for my code of Canon Law. I'll keep my mind occupied with study."

If this amazed the doctors, they were still more astonished to see him quietly reading, all the while they were torturing his body with their cutting and stitching. He gave not a sign of the excruciating pain they were causing him.

Such superhuman fortitude should have been rewarded by a full cure, but it wasn't to be. Father Miguel's pain was, if anything, worse than ever after these first two operations. Everything he ate set his stomach afire, but his cheerfulness never failed. The Sisters who nursed him said they had never seen anything like the patience of this Mexican priest.

The third operation did somewhat relieve his pain, but by now the doctors were very worried over his weakness. If anything could build him up, it should be the fresh air and better climate of the Riviera, the good food and devoted care of the Franciscan Sisters who ran a home for sick priests at Hyères. So he was sent there.

But Padre Pro refused to treat himself as a sick priest. "Do let me say the first Mass in the mornings," he begged the Sisters. "That way the other Fathers may rest a little longer, and, since I can't sleep anyhow, getting up early is no sacrifice for me." When this was granted, the next thing they knew he was assisting at the other Masses after saying his own.

"This won't do, Father," objected the Mother Sacristan. "You are undertaking too much. What with all this running out to give the Last Sacraments, the instructions, and to hear confessions, you really must at least take some rest following your Mass."

"Ay, Mother," he said. "I only wish I could serve all the Masses that are celebrated."

But the Mother Sacristan had been right. His activities worked against his recovery. When they could see no improvement in his condition, his superiors reluctantly decided there was but one solution for their problem with Padre Miguel Pro.

"We feel that your best good lies in your returning to Mexico," they told him in June. "It is possible that the good climate enjoyed there and the familiar scenes may work the desired, yes, miracle. In any case, you'll be with your loved ones and . . . "

"Why wasn't I told before?" he exclaimed. "I'd have offered my life long ago. God doesn't need me to work His good for

Mexico." If this speech seemed somewhat confused to the superiors, it was because they simply either didn't realize or couldn't believe in the terror to which they were returning him. For his part, Miguel had taken their words to mean that they considered his case hopeless. And he agreed that, if he wasn't to live to labor for Mexico's future, he might best become her sacrifice now. For he knew only too well that returning home at this time was to be positively asking for death.

But he explained no further. At once he began preparing for his voyage. The only thing he asked was that, before embarking, he might visit the shrine of Our Lady of Lourdes, and this permission was readily granted. He wrote about his pilgrimage to Padre Magín Negra, whose family had provided the train fare. In this letter, he mentioned that the Blessed Virgin had told him his voyage back to Mexico would not be hard.

7

Perilous Mission

PADRE PRO embarked from Saint-Nazaire in France on the *Cuba,* June 24,1926. He was the only priest aboard, but he matter-of-factly fulfilled all his priestly duties. He did this in spite of the likelihood that some of the passengers might betray him.

The Virgin "had told" him his journey wouldn't be as hard as he had been expecting. Had she also told him that, though the religious were running for their lives from his country, he, a Jesuit, would be able to enter it?

"It was an extraordinary favor of God that got me by the port officials," he was telling the acting Jesuit Provincial two days later in Mexico City. "Strangest of all, they didn't even open my bags in customs."

"Miraculous," agreed Father Carlos Mayer, his superior in the absence of the regular Provincial, now an exile in El Paso,

Texas. "As soon as you are rested from your trip, you'll go on to our Chihuahua college."

Rested? When things were so bad in the capital that the known priests couldn't work at all? So the young, unknown priest (sent home either to convalesce or die "consoled by familiar surroundings") was a godsend. His next order was to study privately for his final Theology examination *while* doing all he could for the nearly priestless parishes. The first thing to happen after his arrival was the official decree prohibiting all religious worship. Now, any priest discovered by the police at any time was a criminal.

"From the first day my confessional was a riot," he said in describing to a brother Jesuit the confusion in which his cruelly heavy labors began. "After the clinic's soft pillows, it was really something, accustoming myself to the confessional's hard bench that I warmed from five to eleven in the mornings and from three-thirty to eight P.M. Twice I fainted and had to be carried out. And at the same time there were all the talks to encourage and counsel our people. . . .

"With the closing of the churches I thought I might relax from the strain of these last days, but anything like that was ruled out by the anxiety of the faithful to go on receiving the sacraments. Talks, baptisms, marriages took every spare moment of the few priests who, thanks to being less known, were able to move about without too much danger . . . "

Nor was this the whole story. In addition to all these duties, he had to take over the parish of a Father Otón who had been forced to flee. He also had a number of places he called his "Eucharistic Stations" where on different days he said Mass and gave Communion.

The dangers for the priests increased when the counterrevolution began. This was the popular movement of laymen, called *Cristeros*, determined to free themselves and the Faith from Calles' savage persecution. Thousands were planning—and arming—for revolt. There already had been some clashes, but so far these had only worsened the terror spread by the government to make life hideous for the Mexican people. The clergy had obeyed their bishop's orders against taking any part in the use of force. But, of course, the nation's religion-hating dictators accused the priests of being behind "the disorder."

In a letter, Father Miguel showed that he was ready, even eager, for martyrdom. "The reprisals all over Mexico will be terrible. First to suffer them will be those who have mixed their hands into the religious question, and mine are in up to the elbows. I am hoping to be among the first, or among the last of 'the selected.' But, as the saying goes, 'Honey wasn't made for the snout of a jackass.' "

At the same time, he knew he must preserve his life as long as possible for its usefulness to the faithful. So, due to the strict censorship of the mails, he signed his letter: "The Miner." His friends would easily recognize the one who had always been the miners' champion. Other times he would close his accounts of the perils in which he was finally serving his own people with the signature "Miguel Enghien." The desperately busy Padre Miguel was living with his now returned father, two younger brothers, and Ana María. More and more of his hours were being spent preaching to office and factory workers, to bus drivers and the poor. To do this and all the rest, he had to keep crossing the sprawling city so fearsomely patrolled by Calles' police. And since he dared not arouse suspicion, he again used his talent for impersonation. Wearing a shabby sweater, rumpled trousers or overalls, and a rakishly tilted cap, with a cigarette dangling from his

He preached to office and factory workers, to bus drivers and to the poor.

mouth, he might have been any fresh young man as, astride his brother's bicycle, he whizzed his way through the streets.

So it wasn't his fault that he returned to the house one noon in December to find the police turning it upside down. "You're under arrest," said one of them.

"But why, for goodness' sake?"

"Isn't your name either Humberto or Roberto Pro and weren't you mixed up in that disgraceful balloon business?"

"It isn't and I wasn't. And neither were my brothers."

"Well, you can tell all that to the lieutenant down at the jail. Our orders are to bring in any man entering this house between twelve and one today." Whereupon Father Miguel was marched off to the Tlaltelolco prison with six other young men, between double rows of policemen.

Rightly he assumed that his brothers' activities for the civil division of the Religious Defense League had become known. But it so happened that they had had no part in the now famous "balloon affair." Earlier in the month, the league had released six hundred balloons over the city in a display which caused wild excitement when it was seen that they were raining brightly colored leaflets. There had been a great scramble to capture the papers with their religious propaganda. The incident had infuriated Plutarco Calles. He had demanded the immediate arrest and punishment of anyone who might have had a hand in the writing, printing, or distribution of the leaflets. Running down the balloon offenders had become the first business of his ten thousand police agents.

Police Chief Bandala himself had searched the Pro house where he had found nothing, of course. Nevertheless, he had left his men there to seize the first arrival among the brothers Pro. That this had happened to be Miguel was very unfortunate, inasmuch as it brought him to the government's notice for the first time.

Upon their arrival at the prison, the seven arrested parties heard the charges against them read out by the lieutenant, and then he added, laughing, "Tomorrow we'll have Mass for you."

This is really bad, thought Padre Miguel. They've identified me.

"Mass?" he echoed along with the other prisoners in a satisfactorily terrified tone.

"Why not," replied the lieutenant, "since one of you is a priest?"

This is very bad, Miguel told himself while they all looked one another over from head to foot, wondering who might be the unhappy priest among them.

"He's a Miguel Agustín," declared the lieutenant.

"Stop!" cried the one of that name. "This Miguel Agustín is I, but I'm going to say Mass tomorrow like I'm going to sleep on a mattress tonight. Someone has just confused my family name, Pro, with Pbro, the abbreviation for *presbítero*."

He could not tell whether his rapid reply had been convincing. Anyhow, he was now herded with the others into the prison patio.

Of this miserable night, he was to tell his Provincial: "We spent it under the open sky. A big bed of cement, meaning the whole patio, was placed at our disposal, together with some enormous pillows, otherwise serving as walls. But there were no sheets, save those the night chill provided. We seven huddled together for warmth because it was bitterly cold. Then, regardless of the guards, we prayed the Rosary and sang softly whatever occurred to us. . . . The next morning they came to waken us with pails of water, but, as we hadn't slept, the first splash had us running about the patio to the laughs and whistles of the soldier-convicts.

"Between us we dug up three pesos, ten centavos, which paid for a pitcher of unsweetened orange-leaf tea that didn't taste like nectar and, being full of frozen particles, left us as cold as icebergs."

Padre Pro was the first to be interviewed by the dreaded Chief Bandala. Since there certainly was no evidence against any Pro in this particular matter, Padre Miguel made his denials and then heard Bandala's proposition.

"Since President Calles is so very furious about the balloons, are you willing to pay a substantial fine?"

"No, Señor—for two reasons," he smiled. "In the first place, I haven't a cent to my name. And secondly, I wouldn't want to suffer lifelong remorse for having supported our present government for even the millionth part of a second."

Somehow he got away with this insulting remark, was released, and in less than an hour: was back to work. Now his superiors were becoming very disturbed for his safety. "We feel we should order you into hiding," Father Mayer, his Provincial, told him.

"Before I've given the Christmas feast at my six asylums and the Good Shepherd orphanage?" he cried in dismay. "I've promised talks, benediction, and general Communion on Christmas Day to each, and to the children, their suppers and toys."

"Well, then, we'll take this up right after Christmas," answered Father Mayer.

How justified was their worry for him became apparent on the twenty-ninth. On that day, the police again burst in on the Pros with orders for the arrest of them all. This time the complaint definitely named "Miguel Pro" as the writer of the leaflets and accused the others of having prepared the balloons. And his statement that "These charges are absolutely false," were so many wasted words.

So, largely for the sakes of the aging Don Miguel and Ana María, he now did slip the raiders a fifty-peso bribe to take themselves off. "Don't imagine, however, that they won't be back," he told the family. "This may be our last chance. We've got to scatter among the homes of our friends pronto." And this they did, taking with them just those belongings they could carry.

Padre Miguel paced up and down the narrow room in which Father Mayer had ordered him to hide. Occasionally, as he passed its only window, he glanced down into the back-yard corral whose one sign of life was a sleepily browsing burro. But he wasn't noticing the scene. While admitting that he better served the Church by this obedience than by any amount of labor, he couldn't help thinking ruefully that he was now as useless to Mexico's harassed Catholics as he would be in a real jail.

What was distressing him most at this moment was the condition of the families of the men who had dedicated themselves to their country's liberation. Because of the wholesale jailings of these men, thousands of their dependents were facing starvation. "If only I could get out of here," he spoke aloud to himself, "I'm sure that by asking for help from our well-to-do Christians I could provide for them."

So far, however, his appeals to Father Mayer had all been answered by the superior's counsel that he use this time in study for his final examination. But he could hardly study when, besides his Bible, he had only two old, long-since revised textbooks. He had twice written the Provincial in El Paso asking that the books he needed be sent to him, but, as he suspected, those letters had never reached their destination.

Suddenly he halted before the window and stared, again unseeing, at the burro as the answer came to him. He could begin the merciful work for the hungry by organizing the handful of his helpers who were still at liberty. Even from his hiding-place he could supervise it, supplying lists of friends who would certainly heed any appeal they knew came from him.

"We are going to build a granary," he told one after another of his former aides who, from time to time, risked visits to his little room. "First of all, we must secure a safe place to store the food and clothing you are to beg of these people whose addresses I've prepared for you. And I'm sure you'll have other names to add to mine. Just think what a relief it will be to our poor friends, whether in prison or still giving their all for the cause, if they know their families are going to eat. To keep me informed of your progress, use whatever means seem safest, and meanwhile I'll be thinking up new lines of action."

And so it was that, within days, Padre Miguel had the consolation of hearing that the generosity of his admirers had provided everything that would be necessary to keep eighteen families over the next two months. It was much, and he thanked God for it, but what was eighteen families among the hundreds and hundreds? Somehow he *must* get permission to return to the battlefield. Surely it wouldn't be disobedience for him to make another try at getting a message through to El Paso.

"Obedience is superior to sacrifices," he wrote his Provincial, "which is why I haven't budged from where I am. However, without pretending to criticize, permit me to say one thing. The people are in tragic need of spiritual assistance. To expose myself, with the needful discretion, as I was doing before doesn't seem to me too daring. . . .

"Oh, I know that there are many who will serve greatly in a future day and it is best that they be carefully preserved. But—I? This isn't humility, Father, nor from a wish to be considered brave. It is merely my conviction before God of my small capabilities. . . . Even if I am discovered, the worst they can do is to kill me and that only on the day and in the hour which God has appointed. You be the judge, Father; and you already know that in everything I shall respect your commands."

Padre Pro was not making this offer because he felt that he might die anyway from his stomach ailment, for he was nearly cured. His postscript to this letter read: "My health is now like bronze. I haven't had a single day in bed. Only very rarely does my stomach remind me that it was operated upon. And in my opinion these times are merely its final protests—after almost eight years of daily pain."

So it was with every reason to believe he might live to lead a normal, pain-free life that he wrote his Provincial pleading for the opportunity to make his sacrifice.

His letter was delivered this time and read with intense appreciation by the Provincial. To Padre Miguel's great joy, his plea was granted. Within a matter of days he was back on the streets again and, if possible, busier than ever.

8

Return To Danger

BACK at the illegal labor of serving persecuted Mexico, Padre Miguel was very happy. The chances he took day and night he counted as nothing, but he followed orders and was very careful. No one knew where he lived. He saw and received messages from his helpers at four different places.

He had only to ask to obtain loans of vacant houses in which to store the begged supplies for his poor. It was space he couldn't do without since the number of families depending upon him had risen to ninety-six. Many of the donations he was nowadays receiving—sugar, coffee, rice, chocolate, even wine and cookies—arrived without his knowing from where they came.

Meanwhile, he was saying Mass and giving retreats— to ladies' confraternities, the bus and truck drivers, office workers. But all this was the easy part of his undertaking. The worrisome part was the constant watching out for the police spies who were always so close upon his flying heels.

One night, upon leaving the services he was holding for government employees, he spotted two men lounging against a telephone pole just outside. Were they waiting for him? Remembering that an attack is often the best defense, he walked right over to them.

"Will you be so kind as to give me a light?" he asked, as he pulled a cigarette out of his pocket.

"You can buy matches in the store on the corner," growled one of them.

"Thanks for telling me. I'll do that," he said, risking turning his back upon them to stroll off to the store.

Just a few feet behind, the suspicious pair trailed him into the shop and waited while he picked up his purchase.

Any chance that this could be a coincidence was disproved when, having returned to the street, he turned one corner and then another without losing them. This was it, all right. Well, he would play it out. Suddenly he made a dash for the first of a line of parked taxicabs.

"Get me out of here pronto!" he commanded the driver, who instantly obeyed. Nevertheless, a glance behind showed him that he hadn't shaken his shadows. They were clambering into the second cab.

"See here," he asked his driver, "are you a Catholic?"

"Sí, Señor, that I am," he heard with relief.

"Well, can you lose that cab that's following us? I am a priest."

The man's eyes shot to his mirror. "I can sure try, Padre," he said grimly.

But it soon became clear that his try wasn't going to be good enough. However fast he went, however many corners he took on two wheels, the pursuers stayed right on their tail. Luckily, another car pulled in between them, so Padre

As Padre Pro said Mass a watch was kept for police spies.

Miguel shucked off his coat, stuck his cap in its pocket, and said, "At this next corner, son, slow down. I'm going to jump for it while you go right along. And let's pray they stick with you."

As the driver braked at the corner, Padre Miguel leaped and, ignoring the wrenching of his leg muscles, managed to be leaning nonchalantly against a tree, holding his coat, when the other cab zoomed past. After all, the men weren't chasing a man in a white shirt.

"Those fellows passed so close to me they almost scraped me with their fenders," he was to say of this incident that might so easily have ended tragically. "And, of course, they saw me, but without dreaming it was I. As I set out limping for home I was telling myself, *All right, son, now we're ready for the next time.*"

It did seem that this brush with danger only made him more daring. Soon he was visiting the hospitals to give Communion secretly to the patients. Then he made even more of a laughingstock of the powers by taking on the prison. Representing himself as a relative or friend of this or that victim of the persecution, time after time he outwitted the guards to give the jailed Christians the consolation of receiving their Lord.

Once again the Pros were together, living three to a room in a reconstructed Panuco Street building where they were hardly better off than the poor that Padre Miguel's project was feeding. It contained nothing but the essentials to existence.

"We are seven and there are five chairs, four plates, four knives, eight beds, but only three mattresses, and a broom—all loaned, meaning given, since it is almost certain that neither we nor our inheritors will return anything," he humorously wrote Father Henry Valley, his good friend and the Provincial's secretary. "In our three police raids they left us not even a cuspidor. But as none of this is needful to getting to heaven, we give it a very low rating."

From the beginning he had been offering his life to Christ for his people's liberation. He couldn't believe he would ever be one of those brilliantly shining fights of the Society of Jesus who he admitted "must be preserved for the future with care." He saw his one big chance for a really important service to his country and Faith as *now*. For mightn't Calles' anti-Catholic mania go too far in making martyrs of prominent and popular religious—figures such as Miguel Pro? If in dying for Christ he might be the means of muting Mexico against this monster . . . ? But it was this glorious privilege which he must resist with all his might, since his vow—obedience—was more important than all his sacrifices and charitable works for his people.

Still, it couldn't be disobedience to hope that his superiors would not, as they had mentioned they might, soon be ordering him out of his country. He thought it permissible to try to persuade them against any such action. He pleaded his case so well in a letter to his Provincial that no more was said about Padre Pro's departure from Mexico.

Plutarco Calles, who was to go down in history as "the Mexican Nero" and "the Turk," was no mere atheist honestly opposed to religion. His deadly hatred for the Church was, first and foremost, hatred for Jesus Christ. His own appalling words, "Three times I've met Christ in my path and three times I've struck Him down," proved his belief in the Lord's existence. He was necessarily, then, the sworn enemy of all Catholic priests. And one of the greatest satisfactions his power gave him was the opportunity to hunt down priests for killing.

It was to make this grisly game easier to win that he had worked out the wicked laws that made the priestly labors "criminal." However, as many Fathers knew by experience, once he had them in his jails, Calles was done with laws, especially the one which guaranteed any Mexican a trial in open court. Their fate really hung upon this man's never-to-be-criticized word.

In fact, the only law of the land which he himself was still prepared to observe was the latter half of that which had been based on the revolution's loudest cry: "Effective Suffrage and No Re-Election." The "Effective Suffrage" part was no more than a cynical joke, for there was no truly free voting in the country. But the "No Re-Election" was lived up to; it might be dangerous for even Plutarco Calles to try to follow himself, that is, consecutively, in office. And that was why he and Obregón had made their deal. To satisfy the law, Obregón would succeed Calles in the office which he would, in due course, hand back to "the Turk." In this way they would share its privileges between them indefinitely.

There were Mexicans who were hoping that this switch to Obregón might improve matters for the Catholics, at least temporarily. They pointed out that, besides being a certainly more agreeable person than Calles, the President-elect was a better psychologist. For while he, too, had no use for religion, he was not likely to risk the hatred Calles had aroused by his fanatical persecution. Obregón really wanted popularity. He was surely too shrewd to go about making martyrs of nuns and priests, too realistic to give the counterrevolutionary *Cristeros* ever more favor in the eyes of the public.

But the *Cristeros* themselves were not so hopeful. They were convinced that, even if he might prefer to soften the religious persecution, Obregón wouldn't risk angering his ruthless partner Calles upon whom his own fortune so largely depended. To the military division of the counterrevolutionary movement, it seemed absolutely necessary to break up this "unholy alliance" now. Only if Obregón were to die before returning to the presidency would Mexico's "No Re-Election" become a fact. And indeed, it would be their one slim chance that some decent patriotic man might head their nation for the next six years.

Ever since May, Padre Miguel had been moving always faster, working always harder to restore Mexico's Christianity by peaceful means. In August he was preaching to the city's chauffeurs—one of whom had saved his life. "I wouldn't trade these strong-spoken, fearless ones," he said, "for all your haughty matrons and sissy *Caballeros.*" He was also instructing converts, preparing the dying, holding Masses "in the catacombs," hearing confessions the clock around.

Though his stomach was now quite sound, the strain was beginning to tell. "If there were a community life here," he wrote Father Henry Valley, the Provincial's secretary, "the load would be lightened 90 percent. But, running to and fro, riding buses guiltless of springs, secretly spying out those who are spying on us, and being threatened with the police dungeons at every turn, one might almost prefer *being* in jail, just to get a little rest."

In September he also took the worrisome final Theology examination on which a trio of Jesuit scholars, Padres Alfredo Méndez Medina, Luis Benítez, and Joaquín Cordero, reported his passable, if not brilliant, grade. After sixteen years of striving, laboring, and suffering on two continents and in five countries, Miguel Agustín Pro had qualified for full membership in the great Society he was to cover with glory.

On September 21, before saying Mass for a community of nuns, be begged them: "Please pray that God may grant me the favor of being Plutarco Calles' victim in the cause of the Faith and to the benefit of our country's priests. My Mass this morning is offered for this intention"

"I cannot tell you how deeply I was affected by that Mass," one of the nuns was to say. "It was celebrated very slowly and I wept the whole time. When it was over Padre Miguel told one of us: *I don't know if it could be my imagination, but I feel sure our Lord has accepted the plan of my offering.*"

And then it was October, that first hideous week of October, 1927, which witnessed the government's assassination of three hundred political opponents. Included among those murdered were the luckless Generals Francisco Serrano and Arnulfo Gómez, who had both dared the impossible by announcing their own candidacies for the presidency. This blood bath had been Calles' grand gesture of loyalty to Obregón, an act which actually assured his own fat future.

To Padre Miguel the horror of this week was a single piece with the rest: his labors, strains, and heartaches to offset the tyranny of Godless men. One of the labors was the carrying home of a six-month-old baby boy abandoned by his parents. The sixth waif he had picked up on his rounds, this was the first for whom he couldn't find another home. But that was all right; Ana María would be glad to care for the little one.

Ten days later Padre Miguel was conducting devotions for all classes of society in Toluca, the State of Mexico's capital city.

9

The Bomb That Backfired

ON SUNDAY, November 13, Padre Pro was back in Mexico City. It was good to relax with his loved ones after the strenuous days in Toluca and before tackling the work that had been piling up during his absence. It was good to be eating dinner with them in Panuco Street and to hear what they had all been doing. The 24-year-old Humberto and 22-year-old Roberto had been busier than usual with their printing and distribution of propaganda for the civil branch of the Religious Defense League. Ana María had been occupied with more than her homemaking for their father and brothers in these almost unfurnished rooms. She had been looking after tiny José de Jesús, the infant for whom Padre Miguel hadn't been able to find another home. She said that he rarely cried and was the best company in the world.

Dinner over and after a romp with the baby, Miguel joined his brothers in a game of catch with an old baseball they had found. It wasn't until after four o'clock that they scattered for their various appointments.

The priest's was with his friends and supporters, the Valezzi family. As he reached their door he heard the newsboys crying an "extra," but, busy with his own thoughts, he didn't listen to what they were calling.

However, from the talk at the Valezzis', he soon knew roughly what had occasioned the "extra." So, when he got back to his house at nine o'clock, Roberto's excited: "They threw a bomb at General Obregón this afternoonl" came as no surprise.

"That is a great pity," replied the padre quietly. "Individual acts of violence are always wrong, and this one, as it was a failure, has achieved absolutely nothing save a sure stiffening of the persecution. Things will just be harder for all of us."

They were thinking this over when a white-faced Humberto came in with the latest edition of *Universal Gráfico*. "Just read that," he demanded, "and then start praying."

Padre Miguel shot him a quizzical glance as he took up the paper. It contained the first detailed account of the attempted bombing. He read that General Obregón's chauffeur had been driving him and his friends, Tomás Bay and Arturo Oreí, through Chapultepec Park around three o'clock that afternoon. Followed by the general's bodyguards, Juan Jaime and Ignacio Otero, in another car, they were killing time until the opening of the bullfights at four. Nobody had noticed the shabby little Essex coming along behind until it suddenly pulled out of line to speed past the guards and the general's Cadillac. But as there had seemed nothing suspicious in that, it was merely habit that made Jaime take note of its easily remembered license number: 10,101.

Somewhere ahead, however, the Essex had swung about—to pass the Cadillac from the other direction. At that instant there was a deafening explosion—then another. Through the blinding swirl of smoke released by these blasts, the Essex, from which came a rattle of pistol shots, began its flight from the scene.

It had all happened so suddenly and the smoke was so thick that, far from getting a look at any of the attackers, no one in either of the general's cars even had seen how many there were. And before taking out after the Essex, the guards drew up alongside the Cadillac, two tires of which had been blown out, to learn how badly their chief might have been hurt. He was sitting by the window on the left side.

Amazingly, he had escaped with nothing worse than a few face and hand scratches from the flying glass. To their worried questions, he had snapped testily: "I'm all right. Just *get* them!"

Pistols in hand and riding the running boards of their automobile, Jaime and Otero wheeled about and took up the chase after the rapidly disappearing Essex.

The car had flashed out of the park and on down the Reforma to the Independence monument where it turned right into Florencia Street. Firing after it the guards tore on until, at the corner of Liverpool and Insurgentes Avenues, it smashed into a Ford. Immediately three, perhaps four, persons spilled out of the Essex and started sprinting down Insurgentes. One of them, being frightfully wounded in the head, was readily overtaken by Otero. A second, unhurt, had been captured by Jaime just as he reached the busy intersection of Insurgentes and the Calzada de Chapultepec. Meanwhile, a traffic policeman, who had been alerted by the shots, laid hands upon a third individual who loudly protested his innocence. The man, who gave his name as Francisco Olivera, declared that he had merely ducked behind a streetcar to escape the bullets and hadn't even noticed the unexploded bomb lying there on the pavement.

These prisoners having been secured, Jaime and the policeman had returned to the Essex to find its interior splattered with blood and a pistol with one empty and one loaded chamber.

In his later declaration at the police station, Jaime stated that he had identified the prisoners he was sure had been in the Essex. The uninjured captive was an Antonino Tirado and the wounded one was Nahum Ruíz, whose injuries included a shot-out eye. Jaime couldn't say whether or not Olivera had been on the scene of the assault.

"Well," said Padre Pro when he had finished scanning the story, "that is that and, as I was telling Roberto, the results are bound to worsen things generally."

"Generally?" exploded Humberto. "But what about us? Or didn't you get it?"

"Get what? It's true that poor Ruíz is one of those on our grocery-receiving list. But what have we to do with his being mixed up in anything like this? And as for Tirado, I've never even heard of him, have you?"

"No, no, you simply don't understand. That Essex with the unforgettable license plate is the trouble. It's the one *I* sold to that Señor González last week for three hundred pesos when the league gave me the Studebaker for the propaganda distribution. Why, Roberto and I have been seen all over town in it for months. And if the registration hasn't been changed, it carries Roberto's picture over the name of 'Daniel García.' Nor is this all. Do you remember my telling you about Señora Montes de Oca giving me a house for the use of those penniless Hernández sisters?"

"How could I forget any of that lady's many kindnesses in behalf of our poor?"

"Well, they were very anxious to secure roomers, and when Luis Segura, whom I've seen driving the Essex since its sale to González, happened to ask me where he might rent a room, I sent him to them. Do you suppose he's bought the Essex and has been keeping it there? And if so, will the Hernández sisters mention my name to the police when that's been discovered?"

Padre Miguel drew a deep breath. "Yes, I'd say they'll likely mention everything they ever knew once Security Chief Mazcorro starts questioning them," he replied.

"Then nothing could be surer than that we're going to be dragged into this mess."

Of all the Pros, only Padre Miguel wasn't staring at the downcast Humberto in horror. In fact, a wry smile was playing about his lips as he mused softly: "So now it comes— and in such an ironical manner."

"Maybe not," put in young Roberto, bravely fighting the quaver in his voice. "Of course Humberto and I will have to get out of here at once and lie low somewhere until they've caught the rest of the bombers. But you ought to be all right. Why, you never so much as rode in that Essex."

"Aren't you forgetting something, Beto—such as *who* the *priest* in this family is?" came the calm reply that nevertheless sent a new shudder through the gathering. "But cheer up everyone," he smiled at one after another of their stricken faces. "Calles hasn't won yet. The three Pro brothers will just go into hiding together."

Security Chief Mazcorro wasn't much concerned that neither General Obregón nor his friends, Bay and Oreí, could supply anything whatever toward the identification of the dynamiters. For even though Nahum Ruíz was in a state of coma in the Juarez Hospital and Tirado hadn't so far opened his mouth, Mazcorro had no doubt of his ability to make Tirado talk. On the information to be extracted from

Tirado, the security department's most ruthless detectives, Valentín Quintana and Álvaro Basaíl, would soon bring in the other two bombers. (The general's guards were now positive there had been four men in the Essex. The third man arrested, Francisco Olivera, had proved his alibi for the hours preceding the assault, and had been released. Thus that left two other men to catch.) Mazcorro and his aides went to work on Tirado.

But amazingly, not to say disgustingly, repeated torturings failed to start Tirado talking. Nor was it even possible to locate the "Daniel Garcia" in whose name the Essex was registered. So Detective Quintana decided to invent a "Ruíz angle." He paid a visit to the dying man's wife, Luz del Carmen, whom he promptly persuaded to take him to the hospital. Once there it did not matter to him that the patient had now lost the sight of the other eye and was, moreover, unable to utter a word. Using his police privileges, he not only pretended to interview the unconscious Ruíz, but remained by his bedside all night. It was Tuesday morning, November 15, when, smilling smugly, he emerged from the hospital with a notebook full of faked evidence.

Meanwhile Padre Miguel had spent Monday and part of Tuesday seeking out a safe place for Humberto, Roberto, and himself to hide until they might manage to leave Mexico. For his own part, he wouldn't have considered such a course, but he must protect his equally innocent brothers who certainly hadn't been called to martyrdom.

By Tuesday afternoon, everything had been arranged. A lady named María Valdés, who conducted a boardinghouse at Londres 22, would gladly receive them. She had asked no questions, but she knew she was offering her hospitality to a priest in flight from the police. So that she might be able to identify her guest the instant he appeared at her gate, the Señora Valdés tore in half a leaflet of the Apostleship of Prayer and gave one of the pieces to the padre's friend.

At seven o'clock the same evening the leaflet was handed back to her by a calm-eyed young man who asked her gently: "You aren't afraid of getting into trouble by taking a priest into your house?"

Her answer was to throw the door wide in welcome to Padre Pro and his companions. Although she was never to ask their names, she heard them calling one another "Miguel," "Humberto," and "Roberto." At first sight she hadn't taken them for blood brothers. From Miguel's *"mís hermanos,"* she had thought they might all be priests—brothers in religion. For this reason she asked if they might not prefer separate rooms.

"Oh, no," replied the eldest gaily, "my brothers will take the bed and I'll be enchanted by the sofa."

Later Señora Valdés was to say: "He got out his chalice and vestments right away and we soon made an altar out of a little bureau."

She was delighted at the prospect of being able to hear Mass in her own home and touched to see the brothers praying together. However, on Wednesday she became worried at the numbers of people calling to see the priest, who received them all and, she suspected, was hearing their confessions.

"Padre," she complained, "don't you think your seeing all these callers is a very risky business? One of them might accidentally give your hiding place away. Should anybody be watching the house, won't this constant coming and going of known Catholics arouse suspicion?"

"Don't worry, Señora," he tried to reassure her. "My visitors are taking all the necessary precautions, and I can't very well refuse them confession. For my part, I fear nothing."

Detectives Quintana and Basaíl couldn't have asked for two more satisfactory days than Tuesday and Wednesday. Based on what the former claimed to have been "told" by Ruíz in his final coma, they had very nearly solved the bombing case. Ruíz' wife having convinced the injured man that Quintana was his brother-in-law, the detective said he had got Ruíz to admit a plot to overthrow the government. Quintana also said that Ruíz named a "Luis" as its leader and said this man could be located at either the Light Company office or an address in La Villa de Guadalupe. Then, after revealing a long list of additional conspirators, Ruíz had warned: "Tell the Pros to watch out. You'll find Humberto at 24A Alzate Street where the bombs were made and which has a broken window-pane."

What had happened, of course, was that the knowledge Luz del Carmen de Ruíz had picked up about her husband's closest associate "Luis," as well as the Alzate address, had been revealed by her under promises that no harm would come to her. It was on no more than this lucky break that the detectives had gathered the additional information, accurate and inaccurate, which Quintana was crediting to a deathbed statement.

It was an outright lie that *anyone* had said Humberto Pro might be found at 24A Alzate. But Quintana realized how valuable this lie would be to his case. In fact, when he and his aides sped out to that address, it was found to be nonexistent. However, there was another clue to "the house where the bombs were made." It had a broken windowpane, and so did 44A Alzate.

The occupants were two young women named Hernández who willingly agreed to an official inspection of their house. Quintanas squad was permitted to examine every room save the one which the sisters themselves could not enter. It was kept under lock and key by their tenant who occupied it only occasionally. However, he was a very nice young man who had come to them well recommended and they were sure he was all right.

But the police were already bashing in the locked door behind which they gleefully uncovered a stock of wicks, tubes, and chemical explosives, everything needed for the manufacture of bombs.

Needless to say the sisters were hustled down to Security Chief Mazcorro. Though they soon convinced him of their ignorance of their roomer's activities, bringing them in certainly hadn't been wasted effort. With the first threat of prison, they had come up with a number of valuable clues.

The lovely lady who had let them have the house rent-free was named Josefina Montes de Oca. She had done this out of friendship for a most helpful acquaintance of theirs, Humberto Pro, the same who had afterward sent them their roomer. However, they simply couldn't believe that Humberto knew what was going on in that room.

Thus, it was on Wednesday, the sixteenth, that Valentín Quintana first heard the name of Pro in connection with his case. Now those who bore that name were in the greatest peril of their lives.

10

A Prize For Plutarco

IT WAS a surprisingly handsome, clear-eyed young man of twenty-four whom the detectives found sitting at his desk in the very respectable Light and Power Company offices.

"You are Luis Segura Vilchis?"

"Sí, Señor. At your service."

"We are security police investigating the Obregón bombing crime."

"Sí, Señor. What may I do for you?"

"We are here to arrest you. You will get your things and accompany us to headquarters."

"With all pleasure, officers."

For at least a year Miguel Pro had been praying that Cod might accept him as a sacrifice for the Faith in his country. If he were to be captured now, his prayer almost certainly would be answered: not because he had known anything whatsoever about the bombing, or that anyone would believe he had, but simply by reason of his being a priest.

Calles, who boasted of having "met" and "struck down" Christ, was not only capable of, but bound to, murder any priest who dropped into his hands under any such favorable circumstances as these. He was also capable of murdering the blameless brothers of that priest, which was the sole reason for their presence at Londres 22. Because, as Padre Miguel had told María Valdés, he feared nothing for himself.

On Thursday morning, the seventeenth, Padre Miguel celebrated Mass before the little bureau serving as an altar. Señora Valdés had slipped into the room with her servants to kneel beside Humberto and Roberto Pro. In testimony given later, the Señora described the stirring event that occurred:

"It was at the moment of the Elevation that I saw Padre Miguel seemingly transformed into a white silhouette, and then, plainly raised above the level of the floor. Later, my servants spontaneously told me that they had also seen this and, at the same time, felt a most unusual consolation."

With the courteous Segura safe and unprotesting in one of the police dungeons, Detectives Quintana and Basaíl tackled the Pro angle of their case. From the information supplied by the Hernández sisters, they rightly supposed that their trail started with the Señora Montes de Oca. Therefore, on this same Thursday morning, they burst in on that lady, to find her hastily packing for a journey. She was being assisted by a young woman with a baby on one arm who claimed to be the wife of a traveling salesman. The young woman seemed in no way worthy of their attention.

Anxiously watched by the mistress of the house, they fell to work ransacking it. Among the papers they collected for later careful examination was one eye-catcher. It consisted of but a single scrawled line: "Don't go to Pánuco. Miguel."

"Isn't one of those confoundedly elusive Pros called Miguel?"

"Uh huh—the one we had in on the balloon deal."

"Okay, let's get busy on the woman."

To their opening demand, Señora Montes de Oca nervously replied: "I am a widow with one young son. His name is José Bolado Montes de Oca, but he isn't in Mexico City at the present time."

"Well, where *is* he?"

Just then the telephone rang, and the frightened lady knew an instant's relief. Answering it would give her time to think. But Basaíl reached it first. At the response to his "Hello," his face broke into a triumphant grin. Because what he had heard in an uncertain voice was:

"Who is this? I want to speak to my mother. Isn't she there?"

"Yes, she's *still* here, José. Where are you?"

"Why, right where she sent me, of course, at Grandma and Grandpa's. Let me talk to her, please."

Basaíl banged the receiver back onto the hook and turned on his most threatening glare. "All right, my *good*, truthful lady," he snapped, "it's off to jail for you, but first we'll have the grandparents' address!"

She gave them the number on Chiapas Street, and the detectives hurried over. There they questioned young José.

"Yes, my mother sent me over here, but, like I said, I don't know why." Under the detectives' bullying, the boy was close to tears.

"Well, you'd better start knowing a lot of things and quick unless you want her to spend the rest of her life in prison!" snarled Basaíl. "Don't you care about that?"

"Of course I do. But I don't know anything to tell you."

"Let's see whether you do. For instance, who's this Miguel whom she's been seeing over on Pánuco Street?"

"Well . . ."

"Yes? Go on."

"Why, he's just Miguel Pro. I guess you must have seen his sister, Ana María, at the house."

Basaíl winked at Quintana. Things were really coming along. "Miguel Pro, hmm. That's not such a respectful way to speak of your mother's friend, is it?" asked Basaíl sternly.

"But I'm not supposed to say he's a priest," wailed the confused youngster.

The detectives were on him in a flash. "Oh, yes you are, and something else you've got to tell us if you ever want to see your mother again is where your Padrecito Pro is hiding himself right now. No tricks either, because you see we *know* you do know his address, don't we?" he appealed to Quintana.

"We sure do, and we also know that your mother's been going to see him there."

"Just to confession, she just took me there to confess!" cried the boy. Then, realizing what he had done, his face crumpled before his hysterical weeping.

"Here, here," said Quintana soothingly, "you've no call to carry on like that. Now you can easily save your mother, take her right out of jail."

"How?" the boy asked chokingly.

"Simply by giving us the address of this place where you go nowadays to get the good padre's absolution."

"Oh—well then," whispered José Bolado Montes de Oca, "it's a sort of guesthouse at Londres 22."

That evening Padre Pro blessed the marriage of a young couple and then had a few words with his hostess. "My brothers are leaving for the United States tomorrow," he told her. "And on the nineteenth I shall be going along to resume my business of souls."

But already Londres 22 was surrounded by soldiery. However, for some unknown reason, no move was made upon the house for nine long and chilly November hours.

At 1 A.M., the last members of the household put out their lights. But it was 3 A.M. before the barking of a dog, followed by suspicious noises from the roof, awakened María Valdés. Thinking it might be someone to see the priest, she went to her window, only to learn that there were twenty or more armed soldiers in her patio.

Highly alarmed, she sped noiselessly to the Pros' door, but no one answered her cautious tap. The sleep of the just, she was thinking as, afraid to knock hard enough to awaken them, she tiptoed on up to the roof. There she found four rifles pointed right at her.

"Careful, lady," warned one of the uniformed men. "Our orders are to shoot on sight anyone appearing up here."

As she was rushing back below, she heard the blows of gun butts against splintering wood, and then, from the priest's bedroom, the command: "Don't move, anyone!" A

Raising his voice, Padre Pro gave his brother absolution.

dozen soldiers, all with drawn revolvers, were already inside. The suspense over, her bravery returned, and she pressed determinedly into the room.

"Repent your sins as if in the very presence of God," a perfectly composed Padre Miguel was saying to his brothers. Whereupon, deliberately raising his voice, he gave them sacramental absolution. In a lower tone he continued: "From here on, we're offering our lives for the cause of religion in Mexico. We must all three pray that God may accept our sacrifice."

Inspector Basaíl moved over beside María Valdés. "Did you realize, Señora, that you were harboring the dynamiters in your house?"

"What I *know*," she retorted flatly, "is that I've been hiding a saint."

Padre Miguel intervened. "This lady is innocent. Leave her

in peace, and do whatever you wish with us." Next he turned to María. "Since they are going to kill me, I am leaving my vestments to you."

"Nothing of the sort," jeered Basaíl. "Why, *you've* nothing to fear from the police inspection!"

Ignoring this sarcasm, the priest went to a small cabinet from which he took nothing but a small crucifix. He kissed it and slipped it into his pocket. He nodded to his brothers that *now* he was ready.

"Aren't you going to bring your overcoat?" asked Basaíl. "It's cold tonight."

"I gave it to the poor."

María Valdés slipped out of the room ahead of them and disappeared. But before they reached the street door, she rejoined them, carrying a serape which she pressed upon the padre. Grief-shaken, she and her maids dropped to their knees for his blessing. When he had given it, no other word broke the sounds of the women's sobs and the shuffling feet of the absurdly numerous escort until they were outside. There, turning for one final look, Padre Miguel drew a deep breath and startled them all by calling in loud, clear tones, "Long live God! Long live the Virgin of Guadalupe!"

After the elaborateness of their arrest, the Pro brothers must have been surprised by the briefness of their questioning upon reaching the police station. Actually, they were officially accused of nothing. Basaíl, however, did take them out to see the bullet-riddled Essex and to chide them self-righteously: "Just look at the result of what you did."

"You are mistaken, Inspector," replied Humberto. "We had absolutely no part in this affair."

Padre Miguel merely smiled. In his face and manner was to be seen nothing save his natural good humor. And he was making friends with the guards even as they were leading him to the underground cell where he and Roberto were to pass the next few days. Nor did he show any disgust for the awful place it was: a damp, dark alley of 4½ x 9 feet, entirely unventilated and filled with a sickening odor. At this time of the year it was also bitterly cold. But the padre only made a little joke about its being dungeon No. 1.

Meanwhile Humberto was thrust into a cell already occupied by Señora Montes de Oca. (Presumably the guards had their instructions to listen to their conversation.)

For the rest, Mexico's prisoners were certainly not indulged at the public expense. They were given neither cots nor food. They slept however they might, and their meals had to be brought in by their families or friends. And no matter how well prepared the food was, it was always an unappetizing mess by the time the guards got through sifting it for concealed messages. Three times daily Ana María brought her brothers their food, but she was not permitted to see them.

Otherwise, the Pros weren't treated too badly. For instance, they weren't beaten nor tortured as Tirado had been until he was seriously ill. The first favor Padre Miguel asked of the guards was that they give Señora Valdés' serape to Tirado. The brothers also divided their food with those prisoners who had too little or nothing to eat.

Perhaps their good fortune in being at first let alone was due to the fact that the authorities' attention had been largely captured by Luis Segura Vilchis. For, of his own will, that unique young man had dignifiedly acknowledged himself to be the author and director of the Obregón bombing plot. "It was I," he said, "who planned and prepared the dynamiting which took place last Sunday. It was for this purpose that I came to the capital from my home town, Piedras Negras, Coahuila. I am a topographical engineer and I personally made the four bombs used, or supposed to be used, from my original formula.

"Three other persons were involved in this conspiracy. One was Nahum Ruíz. Another was the prisoner who calls himself Antonino or Juan Tirado, but who was known to me as Juan Gómez. The former committed himself to assist me last Thursday; the latter only on Sunday morning. I cannot say with certainty whether the so-called Tirado actually threw one of the bombs.

"The Essex car employed in the attack and which, for several days prior to it, was garaged at 44A Alzate Street where I made the bombs, was my property. I had bought it from a Señior José González or, better said, given him the money to buy it. However, I was unaware that the Essex had belonged to

Humberto Pro. Moreover, González, whose address I do not know and whose description I refuse to give, drove the car at the time of the assault. The motive for the attack was political.

"Following the unsuccessful assault, the chase, and the collision, I managed to catch a streetcar on the Calzada de Chapultipec corner where Ruíz and Tirado were captured. And then, like my intended victim, I proceeded to attend the bullfights.

"I am herewith assuming all the responsibility, moral and material, for this attack."

From his story it will be seen that Luis Segura Vilchis was a daring and honest young man. It further proves he had dedicated his life to the *Cristero* counterrevolution and was convinced that only violence would rid his country of the violent men who held it enslaved. Positive that Álvaro Obregón was bound to continue Calles' persecution of the Mexican faithful, he had come to Mexico for the express purpose of killing him. He had failed in his mission, but he was quite willing to pay for that failure with his life.

The melodrama's mystery man, "José González," whose address no one knew and whose description no one would give, unquestionably was an important *Cristero* chief.

Now, Tirado, too, talked for the first time. He admitted having been in the Essex, induced to take part in the plot at the last minute, he said, by Ruíz.

The four men in the Essex had been accounted for. Then what did the police want with *three* Pros? To tell the truth, General Roberto Cruz, Calles' Chief of Staff, who had been appointed to take the evidence, didn't want *any* Pro. He was an intelligent officer who had known too many murderers on both sides of the law to believe for a minute that the Pros were guilty. Anyone with an ounce of brains could see by their faces that they didn't know the meaning of violence. They were brave enough about their fervent Catholicism, yes, or they never would have dared to print "Viva Christ the King!" and "Viva the Virgin of Guadalupe" all over the walls of cell No. 1, nor to pray the Rosary all night long. But assassins, or even politicians? Bah!

Moreover, Cruz knew that there wasn't a shred of real evidence against any one of them. Worse still, he was being driven out of his mind by the large numbers of witnesses who were demanding opportunities to give the Pros alibis for Sunday afternoon. Clearly, too, the padre was a sort of local hero, the most dangerous type of whom to make a martyr. But that was just the thing. Calles hadn't only found a priest, but a *popular* priest upon whom to wreak his wrath. So it seemed there was no chance that the Pros simply would be released for lack of evidence. Under orders from Calles, the questioning of the prisoners went on.

Humberto Pro testified that his first knowledge of the attack on General Obregón had been obtained from the *Universal Gráfico* during the evening of November 13. From the license number, he had immediately recognized the Essex as the car he had recently sold to González and thereafter had seen Luis Segura driving. This was what had caused his brothers and himself to hide from the police. He had known Segura, although but casually, owing to their very distinct activities for the Religious Defense League. His duty was only to distribute its propaganda. Certainly he had never heard anything of a plot involving bombs. All he knew of Ruíz was that he was a member of a group of needy persons to whom he had delivered food. In asking Señora Montes de Oca for the use of the Alzate house, he was merely trying to do a favor for the penniless Hernández sisters. Later, he had sent them Segura in complete ignorance of the latter's reason for wanting a room, because they so badly needed the money.

Then Humberto accounted for his movements during the whole of the attack day.

Next to be questioned was Padre Miguel.

"Oh, yes," he stated unhesitatingly, "I am a priest and a Jesuit." He then went on to say that he couldn't recall ever having ridden in the Essex. "Señora Montes de Oca I know as a most laudably charitable person. Nahum Ruíz I've never known personally, and the only time I ever saw Luis Segura Vilchis was when he happened to attend a baptism administered by myself." He then confirmed Humberto's explanation of why they had sought refuge at Londres 22. And that was all, since he wasn't even questioned on his possible participation in, or knowledge of, the Obregón attack.

Having completed their questioning, the police returned Segura and Tirado to the dungeons. Their fates were now as certain as that of Ruíz who had died at 8 A.M. on Sunday, the twentieth.

But what did it mean that the Pros were also returned to *their* cells? Was General Cruz going to bind them over to the courts for trial?

11

"Viva Christ the King!"

BY SUNDAY evening General Cruz knew that the Pro case was a failure. But because of "the priest angle," he dared not dismiss it nor, on his own responsibility, even send it to the courts for trial. As Ruíz already had, Luis Segura and Tirado would pay for their confessed crime with their lives. And though this left the mysterious José González unaccounted for, he, too, might well be captured any day. No matter. A still surer fact was that the victim Plutarco Calles wasn't going to hear of losing was the Jesuit—against whom not a scrap of evidence existed.

So Cruz had stalled for time by continuing his preliminary examination over until Tuesday, November 22. Maybe in the meanwhile he could find out what Obregón was thinking; he was the only one who just might have some influence with

Calles. Obregón naturally had wanted his attackers convicted, and they had convicted themselves. Surely he wouldn't care to risk backing Calles' priest-hunting mania in a case as politically touchy as this. He, at least, must recognize that even if the Pros came to trial, even if there were a dictated conviction, the public would know it for what it was.

This, of course, rather than the fate of the Pros, was what was bothering the Chief of Staff. From the storm of protests he had received over the long week, he was quite convinced that an illegal disposal of the priest and his brothers would be a disastrous political mistake. He wanted no part in it.

But before he could talk with Obregón, things came to a head. On Monday a jittery Cruz phoned his lawyer, Guerra Leal, to exclaim: "What do you think has happened? The President's ordered me to shoot the Pros—just like that! I told him the investigation isn't finished, nothing whatever proved against them. I tell you I want out of this affair. I'm going to send them over to the garrison, so the executions will have to be there."

Nevertheless, since defying Calles would spell his own ruin, Cruz began trying to soften the news by easy stages. That day's papers printed his carefully mixed-up statement: "The members of the Religious Defense League are responsible for the Obregón attack; especially Humberto Pro and the Señora Montes de Oca in the matter of the house where the bombs were made." But this wasn't enough for the newsmen. They were pestering Cruz to let them talk to the prisoners. Finally, he granted them their first and only chance to do so.

"Are you a priest?" they asked Miguel Pro.

"I am, gentlemen."

"Do you care to make a statement?"

"I wish, gentlemen, to swear before God that I am innocent,

that I had no part whatever in this affair and that I was . .

"That will do," interrupted General Cruz. "Get back to your cell at once!"

The papers of the twenty-second made what they could or what they deemed wisest of perhaps the briefest interview on record.

That afternoon Cruz managed to see Calles and Obregón together. "As I have said, we've got to make an example of this rabble!" thundered Calles.

"But mightn't it be best to give the sentence an *appearance* of legality?" ventured Cruz.

"Forms don't interest me. What I want is the deed."

"What about assigning the accused to the courts?"

"You've got my order and you'll obey it. Moreover, you'll make me a report *in person* when you have."

Still addressing Calles, but with one eye on the thus far silent Obregón, Cruz asked: "Then what shall we do with the preliminary affidavits?"

And now Obregón finally lifted his voice: "Who cares about the affidavits?"

Roberto Cruz recalled the reporters. "Each and every one of the prisoners," he announced, "has been convicted by innumerable proofs, and besides, they have all confessed their part in the attack. It was prepared by seven persons, Segura, Tirado, the priest Pro, his brother Humberto, Nahum Ruíz and two others. Humberto Pro drove the car, Segura and Ruíz each threw a bomb, and Tirado wasn't quick enough to throw his."

"Everything was proved," but at seven-thirty in the evening Padre Miguel was called to make another declaration. On his return to the dungeon, he told Roberto (who still hadn't been identified as "Daniel Garcia"), "It seems the testimony is now finished. They've given me to understand that we're to be turned over to the courts. God grant it may be so."

At about the same time the Argentine Ambassador to Mexico, Don Emilio Labougle, was reassuring his—and Padre Pro's—good friend, Roberto Nunez, that he had been given Calles' "word of honor" that nothing worse than exile was in store for the Pros. And at ten o'clock the lawyer, Guerra Leal, was telling the reporters that the preliminary was now complete, and the prisoners would be turned over to the judicial branch in the morning. This was a strange statement inasmuch as he had already heard from Cruz that, "Calles has commanded me to shoot the Pros tomorrow morning and in the police station yard. He's also insisting upon inviting representatives from all the government offices, the national and foreign press, the photographers. In other words he's going to make it a big show." Perhaps the lie was meant somehow to whitewash the lawyer's friend and client, Roberto Cruz.

As the evening wore on and they were saying their Rosary, Padre Pro was disturbed to see that the guard had been doubled. However, he made no comment until General Cruz appeared in the dungeons at midnight with several other officers and some photographers. "This looks bad," he whispered to his brother. "One of those generals is Palomera Lopez, 'the assassin of the Catholics.'"

Now he, Humberto, Tirado, Segura, and Roberto were all photographed. When it was over and they had lain down again to try to sleep, Padre Miguel again spoke to Roberto. "What do you suppose they're trying to do now? It can't be good. Let us ask God for the resignation to accept whatever is coming for love of Him."

Padre Miguel started up out of an uneasy doze at six o'clock. His head ached, and, as he lifted it from the wet floor to lean it against the wall, he fumbled in his pockets for an aspirin. He could just make out Roberto's figure through the gloom. It stirred and he saw that his brother was awake. He swallowed the pill and said: "I've a feeling that something is going to happen to us today. But don't worry. We'll ask God for His grace and He will grant it to us."

Ana María had been prevented from carrying their breakfast to the prison that morning. So she sent it by two maids of the house where she was staying. When they returned at eight-thirty, they were quite excited. "*Ai*, what a big commotion at the police station, Señorita!" exclaimed one.

"Soldiers by the dozens running all over and so busy trying to keep back the crowd we could hardly get anyone to take your brothers' food," added the other.

For an instant Ana María froze in her tracks, but panic was a luxury denied the Pros. She must hurry, though. "I must go to them," she breathed.

She ran all the way to the jail, to find the street it faced upon indeed swarming with people. She worked her way to the door, but it was blocked by a cordon of police who refused to let her through. However, they were passing in any number of high-ranking officers in full-dress uniform. She spotted Inspectors Basaíl and Quintana elbowing through the crowd and managed to overtake them.

"What is it? What's going on?" she cried.

"We really couldn't say," answered Basaíl.

"Well, I want to see my brothers and they won't let me in."

"All right. Wait here and we'll get you your permission."

But they didn't come back.

The milling of the mob kept sweeping her yards away from the entrance, but she fought her way back again, step by step. The remarks she was hearing on all sides left no question that the excitement was largely over her brothers. Someone said, "The priest and his brothers are being sent to the Islas Marías."

No, no, Ana María sobbed silently. It can't be, not to that hideous island penitentiary.

"To the Target School," contradicted someone else.

"Why there?" she demanded, trying to keep from screaming.

"To be shot, of course," came the giggled reply.

By the time the four ambulances drove up, she was trembling almost convulsively, but it never occurred to her to give up. If she couldn't be at their sides to help her fine brothers, she would at least stay as close to them as was humanly possible.

On the dot of ten, Security Chief Mazcorro tramped down to the dungeons to call loudly: "Miguel Agustín Pro!"

The prisoner stood up and turned to face this very earthly authority.

"Put on your jacket."

As Roberto was helping him into it, the priest asked quietly, "May I know where we are going?"

There was no answer save a slight shrug.

So he squeezed his youngest brother's hand encouragingly and, without another word, walked out of Cell No. 1, the horrid hole his occupancy had glorified forever.

Just as the big double doors were swinging shut at ten, a commotion exceptional even in this nervous throng, broke out about the people. A man was waving a thick document in the faces of the disappearing soldiers and shouting, "*Amparo!*

Amparo!" And immediately that part of the crush nearest the door heatedly took up the cry: *"Amparo! Amparo! Amparo!"*

So Ana María knew, with a deathless gratitude, that some of their brave friends had prevailed upon an even braver judge to sign a restraining order on behalf of her brothers. For that's what an *amparo* was, and is: the most powerful force in Mexican law. Not even Plutarco Calles could ignore his country's *amparo*. It was no mere stay of execution. Once signed by a judge of the Supreme Court, the *amparo* absolutely protects the party or parties it names from not only execution and persecution, but even from imprisonment or exile until his (or their) case can be tried and judgment rendered.

Here it was, bearing the names of the Pros and being presented in time to rescue them from these highly irregular proceedings. But no, not quite in time—since it couldn't be applied out here in the street. And just a moment before, the hour for the guards to lock up had been advanced thirty minutes. So, to her still greater sorrow, Ana María knew that this heroic act had come to nothing because someone had made it known to Mexico's rulers before it could be delivered.

Luis Segura Vilchis had almost boasted of being the planner of the plot, the manufacturer of the bomb, the director of the attack upon Álvaro Obregón. Antonio Tirado had admitted being his willing, if unhelpful, accomplice. Humberto Pro, though innocently, had been indirectly useful in securing the room for Segura. But it was Padre Miguel, unaccused by any witness, never even questioned on *his* participation in the plot, who was to receive the first attentions of the firing squad. And why? Because of nothing but Calles' furious hatred of any Roman Catholic priest. His men well knew who was the star of this specatcle. The appearance of Segura and Tirado could be held up a few minutes. Besides, there was no restraining order at the street door, bearing *their* names.

The prison yard was full of people. There, with his whole staff stood General Roberto Cruz, very cold of face, very hard-eyed. But the fingers holding the cigarette weren't managing to hold it entirely still.

There were reporters, photographers, and more important personages grouped in tight little knots everywhere. After the dungeon's gloom, the padre was seeing them in flashes between his blinked eyelides. Although no one told him where he was being taken, to what he had been sentenced, nor even that he *had* been sentenced, he knew that he was going to be shot.

That this was being done to him, and without a trial, was unimportant. As he walked the length of the compound toward the targets, those repulsive, life-size outlines of the human form drawn upon a shot-splattered wall, nothing he was seeing with the eyes of the body was important. All that mattered was the brilliant vision he was seeing with the eyes of the soul.

He could feel his little crucifix glowing against the palm of his right hand, his humble rosary entwining the fingers of his left hand.

The shadowy figure that was drifting toward him spoke— and became Valentín Quintana, the pursuer —the policeman. "Padre," he said, "I ask your pardon for my part in this."

Ironical? No, just pathetic, as all human failure is pathetic. "I not only pardon you, my son. From my heart, I thank you."

The policeman thinned to nothingness, too, the nothingness of every earth-bound thing. The walking was finished. Before the priest were those outlines shaped like men. Oh, yes, the targets. But *he* was the target. So he turned about to face the knots of people he had passed across a space of sunlit ground.

"Is there anything you wish?" It was an army major —just a voice doing its job.

"To pray."

He was on his knees, crossing himself slowly, folding his arms over his chest as the photographers' cameras clicked. His lips moved in one last offering. Would it be accepted? Such a *poor* thing, merely the life of one imperfect, hard-driven body, to give for Christ . . . for Mexico . . .

He kissed the little crucifix and arose. He shook his head at the proffered blindfold. And then, lifting his arms in the form of the cross, he smiled out upon these unknowing beneficiaries of this sacrifice.

Before his serenity, a shudder ran through the audience which had been brought here to watch him die. The sensation-seekers had thought it would be just another execution of one more stubborn priest, too stupid to seek refuge behind the international line. That was all Calles wanted, wasn't it? To get rid of the sight of them?

And then they heard his voice, firm and clear. But neither was it the voice of triumph. No, there was nothing aggressive in it, just confidence and, somehow, affection. It uttered only five syllables, but *ai!* they were Mexico's best-known. It was the delivery that was different. It would have been less shocking if he had shouted them out, that familiar war cry. He didn't. He just used them for a quiet, kindly assurance:

"Viva Christ the King."

A sharp explosion filled the air with white smoke puffs which rose between the spectators and a crumpled, still form. There it was, but not at all crumpled. He had fallen as he had stood. The cross was now rigid on the ground. No wonder the uniformed man bending above it to deliver the death blow was trembling.

Someone giggled hysterically. Someone said, "It's ten thirty-eight." No one was listening. Their Mexican ears were straining after an echo. Who could help thrilling to that message, as long as men like this kept repeating it, repeating it? But this man was dead. Why? By what right had such a man been *murdered?*

12

Mexico Hails Her Martyr

THE EXPLOSION also stilled the street mob, as all ears strained to catch the sure second report. Segura, they supposed, and then Tirado. When the shot came, Ana María was begging, "Don't, oh, don't, let them make it *three*?" And as the minutes dragged on, she almost persuaded herself that they weren't going to. But they did, so now there must be four.

Four. Well, they had lost their holy gamble, her heroic brothers. Perhaps that was all they had asked. What had *she* asked? What had she expected? Now she would wait for the fifth blasting of those accursed guns—and then . . . ?

In a daze she heard the sergeant's loud shout, "Clear the way there for the ambulances," and saw the great doors swinging open again. Above the crowd's renewed buzzing came other words spoken close by: "Hmm. Only four. They're saving the kid Roberto for Las Islas."

Was it possible? "Oh, please," she was praying now for the thing that had seemed so awful less than an hour before.

She trailed the ambulances to the Juarez Hospital where Edmundo found her with the still-warm bodies of their brothers. Then a firm voice was demanding: "Where are my sons? I want to see them." And into the morgue came that majestic old man, Don Miguel, who had learned about the deaths from the newspaper.

He crossed directly to the slabs, over which he bent to kiss first one, then the other forehead. Next he wiped the faces clean with a worn but snowy handkerchief. When he put it back into his pocket, it was reddened with the blood of martyrs. He stepped back, and Ana María, sobbing wildly, flung herself into his arms. Stroking her hair tenderly, he said, "Daughter, daughter, this is no cause for tears."

They carried their dead back to the Pánuco house, a safe house now. They found it so full of people that there was hardly room for the coffins. These were their friends and co-workers, the devout of every class—from Padre Miguel's chauffeurs and factory hands to unknown ambassadors and millionaires. They kept coming until the whole street was jammed. A far greater multitude than had collected at the police station waited patiently for hours to enter this humble house to pray. Another problem was where to put the flowers that kept arriving by the carloads.

When at 10 P.M., Don Miguel was about to lock his door, he found a half-dozen policemen standing before it. Did this mean still more trouble?

'With your permission, Señor, we'd like to visit the dead."

Sighing his relief, the father made them welcome. Before the coffins they, too, fell on their knees to pray. As they were leaving, one of them said to Don Miguel: "If there is anything we can do, please know you may count on us."

General Cruz had promised that sometime during the night Roberto would be brought to visit his brothers' remains. And in order to give the grief-stricken youth Communion, a certain priest secretly bore a consecrated Host into Pánuco Street. But the promise was broken and Roberto denied these consolations.

At eleven, Father Soto preached a Holy Hour. Then Father Méndez Medina, supervisor of Miguel's last examination, heard the confessions of fifty mourners. The Rosary was recited until four in the morning, when the Fathers began their successive Masses.

At six the door had to be opened again to the workmen who wanted to honor "the laborers' priest" before reporting to their jobs. Whereupon it began all over, the procession of the faithful thousands. By three o'clock, when, all across the city, the hunted priests began praying the Office for the Dead in concert, the neighboring streets were impassable. A special brigade had to be organized to handle the crowd and re-route the district traffic.

The time had come to start the long march to the Dolores Cemetery, so somehow a space must be cleared for the passage of the coffins to the hearses. One authoritative cry: "Make way for the martyrs!" and it was done. At that, too, the multitude fell instantly silent—that is, until it sighted Padre Miguel's coffin in the doorway. Then a thunderous shout went up that reverberated through the streets and across the rooftops of the ancient city: *"Viva Christ the King!"*

Don Miguel admitted the policemen who had come to pray.

With great effort the funeral procession was formed. It seemed that the whole world was determined to touch the hearses with its rosaries or whatever else might thus become a treasured relic. But at last the procession got underway. Miles long, it was made up of four lines of automobiles—two on either side of the thousands who walked four abreast.

Along the entire route the Rosary was recited in unison, with religious songs sung between the Mysteries. At the sight of the hearses, the people congregated along the broad Reforma would drop to their knees and make the sign of the cross. In both directions from the Reforma the streetcars were running empty, abandoned by the passengers who rushed to join the marchers. When at last the procession reached the foot of the grade rising to the cemetery, it was met by the overflow crowd already there assembled. The tremendous swell of the hymn upon which they came together swirled over that other hill of Chapultepec where Calles huddled, nursing his anger at these *unthinkable* proceedings.

But as Padre Miguel's coffin was being borne down into the Jesuits' crypt, the singing and every other sound ceased. Only when the escort reappeared above ground did the enthusiasm of the people burst forth again in a unanimous shout: "Viva the first Jesuit martyr of Christ the King!"

Don Miguel dropped the first shovelful of earth into Humberto's grave nearby. Then he spoke. "It is finished . . . The padre was an apostle; my Humberto an angel all his life. They died for God and are already enjoying Him in heaven. *Te Deum laudamus!*"

How was it that Roberto alone was spared? He had shared Humberto's labors in the cause of religion. The Essex registration carried his photograph—under a false name. He was captured with his brothers.

The Mexicans give the credit to Ambassador Labougle. During the hour which elapsed between the shooting of Padre Miguel and Luis Segura, and the killing of Tirado and Humberto, the ambassador sped out to face Calles and bitterly remind him of his "word of honor" that the Pros weren't to be executed. Whereupon the tyrant, making a show of favoring the diplomat, telephoned Cruz, who reported: "We're now getting ready to shoot Roberto Pro."

"Well, let that one off. We'll just exile him."

The others, he told Labougle, he had had to execute because he couldn't afford an open break with Obregón whose demand it was.

But Obregón did not want the blame either. The temper of the nation had been made much too clear. So he rushed his friend Oreí to Cruz to protest the execution. It seemed that General Obregón "had never been convinced of the brothers' guilt," just as he, Oreí, hadn't believed them guilty.

"In that case," retorted Cruz, "Obregón should have saved them, he being the only one with enough influence over Calles to work any such miracle." Segura's bombs hadn't harmed Obregón, but he would be assassinated just the same—and before claiming the presidency again. Calles, too, would pay for his grisly mistake. Though he would manage to rule a few years through puppet presidents, he was thoroughly hated by the people. Soon it would be *he* who was shunted off into exile, a disease-ridden old man at just fifty-eight.

As prophesied at the Dolores Cemetery that great November 23, 1927, he and the persecution would be the corpses by 1940. Padre Pro's Mexico was done with dictators and army rule. As the country shook off its chains amid a strong religious revival, it could boast of the intercession for its ancient faith of its own twentieth-century martyr.

So Padre Pro's sacrifice had not been in vain. He was beatified by Pope St. John Paul II in 1988 and today, Mexican Catholics—and many others—are confidently begging heaven for his canonization.

Blessed Miguel Pro, pray for us.

www.ingramcontent.com/pod-product-compliance
Lightning Source LLC
LaVergne TN
LVHW021514080426
835509LV00018B/2509

* 9 780999 170687 *